THE SINS OF SOR JUANA

A Play in Two Acts
by
KAREN ZACARÍAS

Dramatic Publishing
Woodstock, Illinois • England • Australia • New Zealand

*** NOTICE ***

The amateur and stock acting rights to this work are controlled exclusively by THE DRAMATIC PUBLISHING COMPANY without whose permission in writing no performance of it may be given. Royalty fees are given in our current catalog and are subject to change without notice. Royalty must be paid every time a play is performed whether or not it is presented for profit and whether or not admission is charged. A play is performed any time it is acted before an audience. All inquiries concerning amateur and stock rights should be addressed to:

DRAMATIC PUBLISHING
P. O. Box 129, Woodstock, Illinois 60098

COPYRIGHT LAW GIVES THE AUTHOR OR THE AUTHOR'S AGENT THE EXCLUSIVE RIGHT TO MAKE COPIES. This law provides authors with a fair return for their creative efforts. Authors earn their living from the royalties they receive from book sales and from the performance of their work. Conscientious observance of copyright law is not only ethical, it encourages authors to continue their creative work. This work is fully protected by copyright. No alterations, deletions or substitutions may be made in the work without the prior written consent of the publisher. No part of this work may be reproduced or transmitted in any form or by any means, electronic or mechanical, including photocopy, recording, videotape, film, or any information storage and retrieval system, without permission in writing from the publisher. It may not be performed either by professionals or amateurs without payment of royalty. All rights, including but not limited to the professional, motion picture, radio, television, videotape, foreign language, tabloid, recitation, lecturing, publication and reading, are reserved.

For performance of any songs and recordings mentioned in this play which are in copyright, the permission of the copyright owners must be obtained or other songs and recordings in the public domain substituted.

©MMI by
KAREN ZACARÍAS

Printed in the United States of America
All Rights Reserved
(THE SINS OF SOR JUANA)

ISBN: 1-58342-061-4

IMPORTANT BILLING AND CREDIT REQUIREMENTS

All producers of the play *must* give credit to the author(s) of the play in all programs distributed in connection with performances of the play and in all instances in which the title of the play appears for purposes of advertising, publicizing or otherwise exploiting the play and/or a production. The name of the author(s) *must* also appear on a separate line, on which no other name appears, immediately following the title, and *must* appear in size of type not less than fifty percent the size of the title type. Biographical information on the author(s), if included in this book, may be used on all programs. *On all programs this notice must appear:*

"Produced by special arrangement with
THE DRAMATIC PUBLISHING COMPANY of Woodstock, Illinois"

Notes from the Author

I started writing this play in 1995, partly as a response to a challenge made by my grandfather, partly as a way of introducing Sor Juana to the English-speaking world. (Her poem "Hombres Necios/Foolish Men" is one many Latin Americans can quote from memory.) I have tried to create a world and language that is both poetic and accessible to today's audiences.

There is a very distinct rhythm to this play. All actors should "think on the line" and only "pause" when it is so written in the script. Please note that a "beat" is shorter than a "pause"; a "silence" is longer.

The "magic" throughout the play—the non-traditional entrances, the wind, the rumblings—are all suggestions of another dimension and hints of Juana's subtle poetic recollection of her past. The suggestions are to expand the play, not limit it to specific productional demands. The level of pageantry and forms of "magic" should be tailored to the creativity, capability, and needs of each production and should always serve the substance of the play.

This play has 10 characters but only 7 actors. The doubling (mentioned on the character page) is for connection between behavior in the Church and in the Court.

Juana was a woman of intense contradictions: vulnerable and strong; independent and needy; poetic and profane.

I truly appreciate your attention to these points.

Muchas gracias,
Karen Zacarías

All translations of Sor Juana's poetry by Karen Zacarías.

Special Acknowledgments

This play would not have come to life without the help and support of the following:

Bill Melton and Patricia Smith Melton; Tom Prewitt, Rick Davis, Kevin Murray and the cast at Theatre of the First Amendment, Washington, D.C.; Kate Snodgrass, Derek Walcott, Diego Arciniegas and the cast at Boston Playwrights' Theatre, Boston, Massachusetts; Jerry Patch, Juliette Carrillo, Lisa Portes, Caridad Svich, Elizabeth Peña and the cast at South Coast Repertory Theatre, Costa Mesa, California; Nancy Benjamin, Norma Wright, Vilma Silva and the cast at AWE and the Oregon Shakespeare Festival, Ashland, Oregon; Jennifer Lister, Karen Sullivan, Karen Fox and the cast at Southwest Repertory, Albuquerque, New Mexico; Ernie Joselovitz and the Playwrights' Forum, Washington, D.C.; Jennifer Nelson, Karen Fox, Gaby Banks, Lesley Bonnet, Sue Mach, Dennis Matthies, Deb Bennet and A4; my friends who read the piece countless times; and last but not least, my family: my parents, my sister Sandra, Bud and Barbara and my husband, Rett.

The Sins of Sor Juana received its world premiere on November 3, 1999, at George Mason University's Theatre of the First Amendment, Washington, D.C. Director: Tom Prewitt, Artistic Director: Rick Davis, Managing Director: Kevin Murray, Artistic Associate: Paul D'Andrea.

CAST

Juana	MAIA DESANTI
Novice	ANDREA MAIDA
Padre Nuñez / Viceroy	CARLOS J. GONZALEZ
Madre Filothea / Xochitl	JENNIFER NELSON
Sor Sara / Vicereine	NAOMI JACOBSON
Silvio	JOHN LESCAULT
Pedro	JOHN BENOIT
Guard	MICHAEL BRYANT
Nun	ANGELA LEE PIONK

PRODUCTION STAFF

Scenic Designer	ANNE GIBSON
Costume Designer	MURIEL STOCKDALE
Lighting Designer	ADAM MAGAZINE
Sound Designer	MARK K. ANDUSS
Stage Manager	MOLLY E. HAWS
Company Manager	KIRA HOFFMANN
Properties	EILEEN DALY

THE SINS OF SOR JUANA

A Full-length Play
For 10 characters (7 actors with doubling)

CHARACTERS

JUANA: Talented, attractive, and temperamental nun. Renown for her writing. Used to be part of the viceroy's court. Age 28-40.

PADRE NUÑEZ: The confessor of the convent and church authority. A lesser poet. Age 40-60. (Doubles as the VICEROY)

SOR FILOTHEA: The Mother Superior of the convent. Age 45-60. (Doubles as XOCHITL)

SOR SARA: Although they are the same age, she is envious of Juana's talents and past. Age 28-40. (Doubles as the VICEREINE)

NOVICE: An aspiring young nun. Age 20-25.

XOCHITL [SO-CHIL]: Juana's maid in the court. Xochitl (means flower in the Aztec language of Nahuatl) is a full-blooded Mexican Aztec. Age 45-60.

VICEREINE: The vicereine of New Spain. Laura is an attractive, dynamic woman. Her affection for Juana disturbs her husband. Age 30-40.

PEDRO: The viceroy's valet. Has been spurned by Juana. Age 35-45.

VICEROY: The temporary ruler of New Spain, appointed for a 6-year term by the king of Spain. Age 40-55.

SILVIO: An intelligent, educated thief, hired to seduce and humiliate Juana. Age 28-35.

JUANA *(beat)*. Nothing... My opinion, Maria.
NOVICE *(beat)*. Why?
JUANA *(ushers her out of the room)*. It's just games for the mind. Just exercise to keep me alive. It's nothing that would interest you. Now go, go.

(A strange wind fills the room. Spotlight fades as candles come to life. NUNS file in chanting in Latin:)

NUNS.
> BREVIS EST AMOR
> EN NOSTRA VITA
> CERTIS EST DOLOR
> SED IN TE MATER
>
> EN TE SANCTA SORROR
> CRESIT FELICITAS

(Repeat.)

(PADRE NUÑEZ, stands C. He begins to chant and lowers himself to his knees and extends his arms so he is shaped as a cross. The NUNS exit. PADRE prays fervently.)

PADRE. *Dios mio,* give me strength. *(Pause.)* Sor Juana, what have you done?

SCENE TWO

AT RISE: JUANA is sitting in her room, writing. She picks up her pen, puts it down again. Picks it up. She reads the words out loud in a hectic, sensual fashion.

JUANA.
>Green temptation of human life
>Mad Hope, a savage golden frenzy
>For open-eyed sleepers that twist and turn
>As treasured dreams smoke and burn
>
>Soul of the earth, bringing birth to the old
>A fantasy of fertile ground
>Dreams break day for a happy few
>Human truth tears dawn down
>
>Glass eyes of green, pursue shadows for
>hope, light, fire
>Twisted sight colors our world and
>heightens the desire.

(In a heightened frenzy.)

>To place my sight in my hands
>I release myself from so much
>
>To "see" only what my palms touch.

(JUANA touches her face.)

>The meter is off, askew.

(She scribbles a line. A loud knock on the door. JUANA is startled.)

What now? Chattering around like a marketplace. Can they never let me be?

(Beat. She hides the poem in a book. No response. JUANA goes to the door and opens it. SARA is at the doorway. JUANA bows.)

Sor Sara.

SARA. Sor Juana—

(SARA enters.)

JUANA. I'm very busy right now. Could this wait till morning?

(FILOTHEA appears.)

FILOTHEA. May God be with you, Sor Juana.
JUANA. Madre Filothea!
FILOTHEA. Did we interrupt your prayers, my child?
JUANA. Prayers are never interrupted when answered. Please, how can I aid you today? Correct a letter? Arbitrate an argument?
FILOTHEA. My child, we are concerned. I am worried. When you are done with your duties and finished with your salon of visitors, you always leave our sight...to spend time alone in your room. We want to be sure that you are not lonely.

JUANA. Dear Madre, as you can see, I hardly get a daylight hour to myself, and when I do, I am never lonely.

FILOTHEA. And yet, you should practice other activities than solitude.

JUANA. Oh! I do.

FILOTHEA. I know.

SARA. Sor Juana, you and I are quite similar... in age... why, we should spend more time together... cross-stitching. You know how to cross-stitch, do you not? We could spend hours like that. You and me... sewing and talking, talking and sewing. Sewing for the glory of the Lord.

JUANA *(beat)*. The last time I cross-stitched, I drew blood.

SARA. Perhaps if you practiced...

JUANA. No! *(Beat.)* Thank you, holy sister.

FILOTHEA. Juana, you've been here for many years and yet, in many ways you are renowned in the province and unknown to us. Sor Sara is eager to reach out to you... to spend time with you, to be your friend.

SARA. Very eager.

FILOTHEA *(pause. Deeply sincere)*. As am I. With age one begins to cherish true connection of mind, of heart.

JUANA *(touched)*. Madre Filothea. *(Pause.)* Why not attend one of my salons? *(Beat.)* You too, Sor Sara, join us for our discussions of philosophy, or mathematics... or our games of poetry.

FILOTHEA. Oh, Juana, I'm afraid we would have nothing to contribute, sitting with all those illustrious and worldly men and women, discussing matters so difficult.

JUANA. You can learn. Use your God-given gift. I have all the books.

SARA. So many books.

JUANA. Yes, and all of them have something to teach. Oh, where to start? Aesop? Aristotle?

SARA. Your favorite books would be best, no?

FILOTHEA. Could I suggest, perhaps this one? *(Points to a book on the shelf.)*

JUANA. Oh! Sophocles...a wonderful choice...his plays sing off the page and onto the stage. *(JUANA hands the book to FILOTHEA. FILOTHEA hands it to SARA.)*

FILOTHEA. And that one?

JUANA. Ah, Copernicus. *(JUANA hands the book to FILOTHEA who hands it to SARA.)* The moon, the stars, the earth all in your hands. Although, *(Beat—in a whisper.)* Galileo has a more logical argument, placing the sun as the center of the universe...with the earth rotating— *(SARA and FILOTHEA, scandalized, cross themselves. JUANA quickly jumps in and does the same.)* And however mistaken, these theories bring us closer to God by contemplating the beauty of His labor.

FILOTHEA. Amen. *(Looks at the books.)* Well, these are a start...

SARA. But Madre Filothea, this book on her table...?

JUANA. The one that I am reading...would enchant you. It is poetry. Góngora. Please. *(Hands the book to SARA.)* Knowledge is the best weight to carry.

FILOTHEA. So true.

SARA. Sor Juana, I care to see that one. *(She takes a book.)*

JUANA. Certainly.

SARA. And, if Madre Filothea does not mind, this one.

JUANA *(realizes what is happening).* With all due respect...

SARA *(takes them)*. And those over there. And the one on the chair!

JUANA. Why are you are taking all my reading away? *(Pause.)*

FILOTHEA. Sor Juana, please, do not make this more difficult than it is.

JUANA. All my books!

SARA. You still have the Holy Bible.

JUANA. Dear Mother, I thought you understood!

FILOTHEA. Sor Juana, believe me, I am doing this for your sake.

JUANA. Padre Nuñez will be outraged and sickened by your misguided actions. He will decry every moment that has transpired here.

FILOTHEA. Sor Juana, forgive us, but we are acting at Padre Nuñez's behest.

JUANA. That's not possible. Many of these books are gifts from him. *(Pause.)* I must see el Padre...

FILOTHEA *(as SARA and FILOTHEA crowd the doorway)*. I'm afraid el Padre is very occupied right now.

SARA. He's very busy.

JUANA. He is my confessor!

FILOTHEA. I know, my dear. *(They hurriedly walk out with all her books. JUANA calls out after them.)*

JUANA. And if I cross-stitched?

FILOTHEA *(comes back; pause)*. Afternoon cross-stitching with the convent sisters would definitely warrant the Father's attention.

JUANA *(beat)*. Filothea, you never intended to read.

FILOTHEA *(pause)*. If I must deceive you to save you, so be it. It is my sin and cross to bear.

Act I THE SINS OF SOR JUANA 17

SARA *(has returned)*. Sor Filothea, we should remove the writing from her desk.

JUANA. You wish to have that too?

FILOTHEA *(sighs)*. It would be best. *(JUANA hands her the paper.)* Thank you.

SARA. The pen? The desk still holds the ink! She could still write. We must prevent what we can.

JUANA *(hands SARA the feather pen and ink bottle)*. It is yours. God be with you.

FILOTHEA. This is for your own good. I would never hurt you, Juana. You see that, don't you?

JUANA. I am not blind.

FILOTHEA. You will then see the charity of our actions.

JUANA. I am not blind.

SARA *(as she and FILOTHEA begin to leave)*. God be with you, Sor Juana.

FILOTHEA. God bless you, my child.

JUANA. Sisters?

FILOTHEA. Yes?

JUANA *(pause)*. You have forgotten to take the candle.

(Lights out.)

SCENE THREE

AT RISE: *SOR SARA and the NOVICE are cross-stitching.*

SARA. He is very upset. Madre Filothea says she's never seen el Padre like that.

NOVICE. *Dios mio.*

SARA. And he asked... no, begged, that we help him... help him to save Sor Juana's soul. And I was honored to be included. Our Sor Filothea, I most confess, was less enthusiastic. Age, I'm sure. It's not an easy thing you know... saving a soul... especially one like Sor Juana's.

NOVICE. But Sor Juana is very nice. A little strange, but nice.

SARA. I thought she was nice too, years ago, when she first arrived. We were placed in the same room. She stayed up half the night, reading, rustling papers, but I tried... I truly tried... to befriend her. *(Beat.)* She asked to be moved. To be by herself. *(Beat.)* It was for the best. Sor Juana is not as respectable as she sets herself up to be.

NOVICE. She is a sister of the church.

SARA. What I mean to say is that she had humble beginnings. She is a natural child.

NOVICE. No father?

SARA. Shhh!

NOVICE. But then how would they allow her here?

SARA. Thanks to the Vicereine's influence.

NOVICE *(excited)*. Ay! So it is true! Juana was a part of the Vicereine's court!

SARA *(cold)*. Yes. And now she is a member of a better court. The court of God.

NOVICE. Of course. Blessed are we all.

SARA. Be careful. You are about to miss a stitch.

NOVICE. Sor Sara? How did a poor, illegitimate girl end up knowing the Vicereine?

SARA. When she was twelve, she dressed like a boy, so she could try to study at the university. Can you believe that?

NOVICE. I don't understand.

SARA. Word got out that there was a child as intelligent as forty men. So the Viceroy and Vicereine brought Juana to the court...and sat her in front of forty universitarians who fired questions at her. And she responded.

NOVICE. Just like the boy Jesus in the temple! *(Icy pause.)* Forgive me. *(Longer pause.)* Sor Sara, why did she come here?

SARA. Indeed. Why?

NOVICE. Why?

SARA. Dear Maria, you know that the past does not matter here.

NOVICE. Of course. Forgive my impertinence.

(Sew in silence.)

SARA. It had something to do with a man.

NOVICE. A man?

SARA. Two men, actually. *(SARA crosses herself. The NOVICE does as well.)*

NOVICE. May the Holy Sainted Blessed Virgin protect us all.

SARA. Yes. Especially those among us that are not.

(Enter JUANA; NOVICE does not see her.)

NOVICE. So what happened? Why did she come here?

SARA. Dear Maria, why do we all come here? For God. There is no other reason. Sor Juana is here for God. Right, Sor Juana?

NOVICE *(turns, surprised to see JUANA)*. Sor Juana.

SARA. Did you not join this convent to give yourself to God?

JUANA *(plainly)*. I am here to cross-stitch. *(JUANA sits, nods to NOVICE. NOVICE nods back.)*

SARA. A holy pursuit. Hopefully you will learn your place and role in the process. I pray for you.

JUANA. Thank you. I'm certain God sees this and will take note of your actions.

SARA. Certainly, for He sees all. And knows all.

JUANA. I pray He does.

SARA. You doubt?

JUANA. Doubt?

SARA. Question?

JUANA. No. *(Pause.)* I sew.

SARA. And what are you sewing? *(SARA and NOVICE go over. NOVICE gasps.)* Sor Juana, What on earth are you doing???

JUANA. My cross-stitching.

(Enter PADRE AND FILOTHEA. SARA sits down.)

PADRE. What a sight to behold. Miracles do happen. Good day, Sisters.

SARA & NOVICE. Good day, Reverend Father

JUANA *(stands)*. Padre, I am so happy to see you.

PADRE. I'm pleased to find you here as well.

JUANA. Padre, I believe there's been a terrible mistake, all my books and pens—

PADRE. Sor Juana, be SILENT and SEATED. Now! *(SARA and NOVICE begin sewing. JUANA sits down. To FILOTHEA.)* The holy sisters are working assiduously.

FILOTHEA. Yes.

Act I THE SINS OF SOR JUANA 21

SARA. As always. Even Sor Juana is a skilled artisan.

PADRE. Really?

NOVICE. Oh, but my work is more complete. Take a look.

FILOTHEA. Ah! St. Sebastian being martyred by the infidels. Arrows. Lovely!

PADRE. Sor Juana, what are you creating? *(JUANA hands over cloth. PADRE takes the cloth.)*
> What wild ambition drives us
> To forget ourselves, our past?
> We spend a long time yearning
> While our lives quite barely last

JUANA. For you, Padre. The first verse I wrote under your tutelage. Remember?

PADRE *(pause; angry)*. Filothea, I thought you understood!

FILOTHEA. I'm trying, Padre! Just the fact that she is here, with her Sisters...

JUANA. Padre, careful, remember your heart!

PADRE. Remember yours, Juana, and do not direct a word to me. Sisters! What do you think of this? *(Points at the cross-stitching.)*

SARA. I am praying for Sor Juana's soul.

PADRE. Maria, what do you think of what Sor Juana has written?

NOVICE *(pause)*. Me? Her style leaves room for improvement.

PADRE. In what way? The rhyme is perfect, the meter contained...

NOVICE. She should use the double-stitch for letters.

PADRE. Ah! I see. Very good. Sor Juana, next time you threaten the foundations of this establishment, make sure you use a double-stitch pattern.

JUANA. Padre, what has happened?

PADRE. There is a publication of your work, Sor Juana.

JUANA *(pause)*. Really? ... It exists? You've seen it?

PADRE. I've seen it. Do you know the title? *(JUANA shakes her head. Beat.) Verses and Essays by Sor Juana Inés de la Cruz, the 10th Muse of Mexico, Phoenix of Poetry...*

JUANA. *Dios mio. (Beat.)* A bit excessive, no?

PADRE. Why was I kept in the dark about this?

JUANA. Padre, I am almost as surprised as you.

PADRE. No. I thought all your poems were on godly matters. Only two poems about our Lord and the rest: Romantic poems, carnal poems. How? When? I am your mentor.

JUANA. But, Padre, I showed you the sonnets on friendship and one of the poems on love. *(Pause.)*

FILOTHEA. Is that true, Padre?

PADRE. I never imagined she would allow them beyond these walls. Am I published? No! I know my role. I have discipline. Nothing I do, say, write, interferes with my mission...my respect for the church and my devotion to God.

JUANA. I do not see how poetic exercises by as simple a woman as myself could possibly threaten the vast power and glory of our church.

PADRE. My work is to ensure that you serve God.

JUANA. And if God has chosen for me to serve in this manner?

PADRE. You have chosen this! YOU chose this. Not God!

JUANA. Reverend Father, you knew the day that you allowed me through these doors that I came here to write and study.

PADRE. I quote you. "Heat and Heart, trembling in the dark." I quote you.

SARA. But how ...

PADRE. "The agony of loving, of feeling, of thinking is the Divinity I desire and know," I quote you.

FILOTHEA. God have mercy!

SARA. Padre!

PADRE. "My breast, my skin, my heart, shine with the delicacy of your touch," I quote you.

NOVICE *(almost impressed)*. Sor Juana!

JUANA. "Let him kiss me with the kisses of his mouth— My Lover is to me a sachet of myrrh, resting between my breasts," I quote—

FILOTHEA, NOVICE & JUANA. "The Song of Solomon."

PADRE. Enough! I've been called before the Inquisition.

FILOTHEA. Padre! No!

JUANA. The Inquisition? *Dios mio*. For my poetry?

PADRE *(pulls out the letter JUANA wrote to the bishop. Beat)*. I wish I had known you had other mentors. The bishop is a very learned man.

JUANA *(pause)*. Forgive me, Padre. I should have told you. The Bishop of Puebla. He contacted me with a series of theological questions.

PADRE. And he contacted the Inquisition with your series of letters.

JUANA. *Dios mio*.

PADRE *(reads from the letter)*. "It is possible that without us, God would not exist. Perhaps He suspects He is but a memory, a construction of thought, inside the mind of men and women." I quote you. *(Long pause.)*

JUANA. It's rhetoric. There is a context if you ...

PADRE. For years I have defended your work, your studies, to skeptical clerics; I believed that learning and writing were invaluable tools for a woman of God. But your weakness has proven me wrong. You cannot handle your learning, look where it has led! Blasphemy! These are troubled times, the rains, the ruined crops, the native rebellions. God's wrath is upon us. The Inquisition is relentless and your hunger has put all of us, ALL OF US, at risk. God forgive me for indulging your talent. I forgot to mentor your soul. Sor Juana, do you love God?

JUANA. Padre, you know my answer.

PADRE. Do I?

JUANA. Yes. *(Pause.)* I love the Lord.

PADRE. Again.

JUANA *(breathes)*. I love the Lord.

PADRE. Say it with your soul!

JUANA. I love the Lord! *(Long pause.)*

PADRE. I made exceptions for you, but you have forsaken my tolerance and abused my trust. You have been living in religion without religion. Save yourself, Sor Juana. Renounce. Pull out every single word you have stitched onto that cloth. Now.

JUANA. Lope de Vega, Calderón, Góngora are all published writers and men of the cloth. Man has always...

PADRE. You are not a man!

JUANA. I know.

PADRE. Until you see the grave errors of your ways, until you destroy this stitch... I will not see you. I will not accept your confession.

(FILOTHEA, SARA and NOVICE are shocked.)

Act I THE SINS OF SOR JUANA

JUANA *(shocked and scared)*. Padre...
PADRE. I will not recognize you, nor bless you. Nor hold your hand in the search for God. *(Beat.)* I will recommend ex-communication.
JUANA. Please, no!
FILOTHEA. God have mercy!
PADRE. Remember what you did that drove you here.
JUANA. Padre, remember what saved me.
PADRE. My daughter: please. Pull the thread from the cloth and renounce the words that hold you captive from God. I beg you.

(Pause. JUANA, moved by PADRE's plea, tacitly takes the cloth and truly attempts to destroy it. She looks at the cloth, slowly shaking her head. She doesn't understand herself why she is refusing.)

JUANA *(softly)*. No.
PADRE. You are dead to me. *(Beat.)* Take Sor Juana back to her room. *(Coughs.)*
FILOTHEA. Father, your heart.
PADRE. What heart? *(Coughs.)* God will grant the time He sees fit. *(Pause.)* May God save you, Sor Juana.

(PADRE exits. SARA and NOVICE stare at JUANA. JUANA is devastated.)

NOVICE. It's but a cloth with thread.
SARA. Shhh!
FILOTHEA. Come, Sor Juana.

(A dazed JUANA walks with FILOTHEA back to her room. SARA and the NOVICE follow.)

JUANA. Madre Filothea, why has el Padre abandoned me?

FILOTHEA. Perhaps because you have abandoned God.

JUANA. Have I?

FILOTHEA. Sor Juana, in this lifetime, it is more important to be humble than to be right. It is more important to accept than understand. It is a lesson you have always failed to learn. The rest of us... we don't think we are important enough to demand differently. You do and God forgive you for your crime.

JUANA. Which one?

FILOTHEA *(becomes upset)*. Knowledge is not always wisdom! You should have written only for the eyes of God. It is your pride, Sor Juana. What will become of you, my child? And what will become of us? Why do you break our hearts this way? *(To SARA and NOVICE.)* Go on with her. *(Exits.)*

SARA. This will give you time to think. Your cell, Sor Juana. Good night. May your memories remind you of who we really are. May the angels protect your sleep. I will pray for you. *(Exits.)*

NOVICE. I liked the poem... despite the stitching. *(Exits.)*

JUANA *(the door closes)*. What a stupid woman I have become. Forgetting that ignorance is always the cleverest way. I have defied my Father. I have brought the Inquisition upon this House!!!! *(Pause. Walks around the room.)* God, why instill curiosity in women, and then punish them for having it? *(JUANA grabs the crossstitching but can't destroy it. On her knees.)*

> If you can't make me understand, then help me to be good.
> They say I sin when I learn... and yet how can I reasonably stop? If it is true that I should not learn, then teach me to hate knowledge...
> Teach me to respect ignorance and silence. To abhor the musicality of words and the beauty of worldly ideas.
>
> Teach me, to accept the path as it is and
> To submit to the authority of the narrow mind...
> And teach me, above all, to really want what I am asking for... because, Lord, in all truth, I prefer this prayer go unanswered.
> Amen.
>
> What a fool I am. Cursed by Eve's affliction. Knowledge should lead me to true union. How did I end up so alone? I thought coming here would give me some type of freedom. But I'm trapped. Trapped.

(Long silence. A noise comes from the chest in her room. JUANA leaps to her feet and runs to the chest.)

JUANA. I've gone mad.
XOCHITL. Let me out! Let me out! Auxilio!

(JUANA unlocks the chest. XOCHITL, her old maid from her days at the court, emerges, she pulls some cobwebs off.)

JUANA. Xochitl! Oh dear goodness.

XOCHITL. *Mi'jita. (Coughs.)* Dusty in there.

JUANA. Xochitl!

XOCHITL. Juanita!

JUANA. Ay, I've missed you. *(Throws her arms around XOCHITL and starts to cry.)*

XOCHITL. *Ya. Ya. Pobrecita.*

JUANA *(calms down and pulls away)*. What were you doing in there?

XOCHITL. You put me there, *mi'jita*. Don't you remember? I'm in there with a lot of other memories.

JUANA. *Ay, Dios mio. (Starts to walk around the room.)* I know why you are here. Pray for me, Xochitl. Because I can no longer pray for myself.

XOCHITL. Pray for you? All right. In the name of the Father, Quetzalcoatl, and the Holy Spirits, Amen. *(XOCHITL crosses herself incorrectly.)*

JUANA. Xochitl. *(JUANA crosses herself correctly.)* It's in the name of the Father, the Son, and the Holy Ghost.

XOCHITL. Fine. I know. I just don't want to seem partial to anybody up there.

(The young VICEREINE enters from the closet in a splendid, alluring dress.)

VICEREINE. Juana! Juana Inés! Oh, there you are.

JUANA. The Vicereine. Mi señora.

(JUANA and XOCHITL bow. VICEREINE comes up to JUANA and kisses each cheek.)

VICEREINE. What's the matter, my little one?

JUANA. I had forgotten how beautiful you were!

VICEREINE. It's your beauty. It is your reflection you see in my eyes. Although you are not wearing the dress I bought for you.

(JUANA looks down at her black habit.)

XOCHITL. Mi Doña, you know how difficult it is to make her look out after herself.
VICEREINE. Ay no. Don't tell me she cut her hair off again. You silly goose! Did you cut your hair again?
JUANA. But we're supposed to.
VICEREINE. Xochitl! You promised you wouldn't let her near the scissors.
XOCHITL. I didn't, mi Doña. But she's like a wild turkey.
VICEREINE. Well, take that silly sheet off her head. Let us inspect the damage.
JUANA. But my habit is a sign of humility and...
VICEREINE. Off! Off!

(XOCHITL removes the veil, JUANA's long hair cascades down.)

JUANA *(surprised)*. I have hair!
XOCHITL *(relieved)*. She didn't do anything.
VICEREINE. Oh! Unscathed by your own ideas! *(Laughs.)* I'm sorry, my dear. It's just you gave me quite a scare when I saw you all covered up. Remember that time you came to me and you had cut your own hair? *(Laughs.)*
JUANA. *Si.*
VICEREINE. You said "A head adorned by hair and no knowledge is an ugly sight."
JUANA. It is.

XOCHITL. Tufts sticking out in every direction. She looked like a hen that had survived a rooster fight.

JUANA. I was fourteen. I was trying to learn Greek.

XOCHITL. And every time you stumbled, off came a tuft of hair.

VICEREINE. And this drab clothing?

JUANA. Take it off! Off! Off! ...

XOCHITL. Patience, *mi'jita*. *(XOCHITL unhooks JUANA's habit.)*

VICEREINE. Yes, take it off!

XOCHITL. Patience, mi Doña. All good things take time.

(XOCHITL removes JUANA's habit, revealing a colorful, beautiful, alluring gown. JUANA looks at herself, touching her hair, her body, her gown. The crucifix is lifted.)

JUANA. Look at me. *(The room becomes a colorful palace room. A fanfare is heard.)* Dios mio!

VICEREINE. Now, that's what I like to see. That dress is so pretty on you. *(VICEREINE places her hands on JUANA's hips and guides her to a long mirror. She stands right behind JUANA as she looks at her own reflection.)* Now, tell me, what do you see?

JUANA. It's you and it's me. And yet, it's not. *(She rearranges the dress...pulls off some frill until it's "her way." Like a young girl.)* There, that's better. Oh, I like this dress. It makes me look pretty, doesn't it?

VICEREINE. No...you make the dress beautiful.

JUANA. But underneath, there's an angry old spirit.

(VICEREINE and XOCHITL look at each other, VICE-REINE erupts in laughter.)

VICEREINE *(throws her arms around JUANA)*. You are so funny. So funny. I love it when you say things like that. *(Takes her hands and they both spin around.)* Juana is an angry old spirit, Juana is an angry old spirit! An angry old spirit that looks good in a dress. *(Stops spinning and then hugs.)* Did you hear her? This country is so wonderfully ... odd. Isn't this a funny land, Xochitl?

XOCHITL. Yes. Ha-ha. Only laughter in our bellies.

VICEREINE. Grumpy old woman.

XOCHITL. Juana is right. She's the oldest person in this whole palace. But she just doesn't have enough experience to be her true age. Not yet.

VICEREINE. You Mayans say the strangest things.

XOCHITL. Mi Doña, I am Aztec.

VICEREINE *(laughs)*. Regardless, I want Juana to turn into an old woman by my side, so we can be two cranky ladies together.

XOCHITL. But the Viceroy just announced that all ladies without noble lineage must leave the court.

JUANA. And there's only one "lady" with no title.

VICEREINE. I don't think he knows how much Juana means to me.

XOCHITL. I think he does.

JUANA. Did you speak to him?

VICEREINE. Oh, why speak to that man these days? He says his hands are tied ... Spanish decorum must be kept even in her colonies. HA! He who has probably spawned a little colony of bastards. Oh, nothing like you. *(Beat.)* Juana, I want you to stay.

JUANA. So do I, and I wrote a persuasive letter to the Viceroy listing all the reasons why I should.

XOCHITL. Twenty-five pages long.

VICEREINE. I know. *(Pulls it out.)* Thank God I got to it before he saw it. Juana, you are no longer a child. You cannot directly ask for things.

JUANA. He needs to hear me.

VICEREINE. Beg forgiveness, not permission. An aristocrat always employs more subtle and successful solutions!

JUANA. Hence my problem.

VICEREINE. My dear, you weren't born with nobility—

JUANA. And I'm certainly not going to marry it. *(Long pause.)* No! There must be a better alternative.

VICEREINE. If you marry my uncle Fabio, you will always be a part of the household.

JUANA. Don Fabio?

XOCHITL. That sore, dry, cranky man?

JUANA. I have no dowry...

VICEREINE. I have offered Don Fabio a dowry in your name. And now he wishes to ask for your hand in marriage.

JUANA. Mi señora! You should have spoken with me before...

VICEREINE. Juanita, it's the simplest way. You are the most wonderful friend I've ever had.

JUANA. Then why marry me to Don Fabio?

XOCHITL. That man has never laughed in his life.

VICEREINE. He can provide.

JUANA. Señora, you told me that marriage was the devil's hunting ground.

Act I THE SINS OF SOR JUANA 33

VICEREINE. Oh, only on the bad days. Besides, Don Fabio is nothing like the Viceroy.

XOCHITL. True. The Viceroy is handsome.

VICEREINE. Fabio is Fabio.

XOCHITL. Is he sickly? Could he die soon?

VICEREINE. He's a healthy man with many years ahead.

XOCHITL. Decades and decades of boredom.

JUANA. There must be another way.

VICEREINE. Juana, my words are weak and ephemeral and subject to my husband's whims. Marriage is the only protection and insurance you can have.

JUANA. But I don't love him.

VICEREINE. How fortunate. Believe me, the less you love him, the better.

JUANA. But, I really don't...

VICEREINE. Would you rather we never see each other again?

JUANA. No! No...it is simply that...

VICEREINE. Listen, Juana, it's time that you learn a little about being a woman. Compromise. Never aim to win and you will never lose... negotiate...yield... and you will get further than you think. Do not try to conquer...it will make others want to destroy you. Men who conquer win or die; women who compromise always survive.

JUANA. Marriage is not...

VICEREINE. You're frightened, are you not?

JUANA. Yes! No! I don't know! Forgive me, señora, but I've heard that men are like farmers...they spread a little seed and then think they own the land.

XOCHITL. And the plow, and the horse, and the—

VICEREINE. Allow them to think they own you. There's power in passivity, my dear. Strong women are like the moon; they quietly glow as they control the tides. And Fabio is just a man. Men, you know, they don't bite... not often... and if they do, a nibble can even feel pleasant, sometimes.

JUANA. If he nibbles, I'll bite!

VICEREINE. No! No! Let him do the work. He's the man.

JUANA. I don't follow.

XOCHITL. You shouldn't—

VICEREINE *(silences XOCHITL with a harsh look and sends her to hang up the nun habit)*. It is all so simple. Night falls and you and he are alone. He approaches you and takes your hands *(VICEREINE takes JUANA's hands. A sexual undercurrent.)* and looks into your eyes and says, "You are so beautiful. Your eyes, your hair, your mouth, your breasts. Let me feel how beautiful you are." Then he takes his hands and traces the outline of your form. *(VICEREINE traces JUANA's body.)* Then he takes your face in his hands *(VICEREINE holds JUANA's face.)* and looks longingly at your mouth...

JUANA *(leans over and kisses VICEREINE on the mouth)*. And kisses you? *(Pause.)* Is that what you wanted... to say?

VICEREINE. Yes. No. *(Flustered pause.)* Do not give, just allow him to take. Enjoy if you can... and if you can't...

XOCHITL. Do not do it!

VICEREINE. Think of something else... like a poem, an errand... A good friend.

XOCHITL. Dishonesty.

VICEREINE. Honesty only brings heartbreak and defeat.

JUANA. What if he wants to take my writing?

VICEREINE. Juana, we have all delighted in your exquisite wit and words... but you are sixteen, and it is time to

Act I   THE SINS OF SOR JUANA   35

leave childish pursuits behind. A poem does not put food in your belly, or a roof over your head. A husband will not want you to be distracted from your important duties.

JUANA. I will not give up my writing or studies.

VICEREINE. Perhaps your husband will give you permission to read your work to the ladies court.

JUANA. Give permission?

VICEREINE. Sometimes. No man likes to be publicly outdone by his wife. That much is clear. But privately, secretly, you can always find a way to read and put your thoughts on paper.

XOCHITL. It is not enough. Juanita's spirit will burst.

VICEREINE. Xochitl, be quiet! Juana, the choice is yours. Perhaps you prefer to go back and work on your knees from dawn to dusk on your dead mother's farm. Or choose to leave to become a concubine to wealthy men. Or you can nobly die of hunger as you write a poem in the dirt. Or *(Pause.)* marry a decent man... and remain a part of the court.

JUANA *(pause)*. If I marry... I must compromise.

VICEREINE. Bravo!

JUANA. And then, so must he.

VICEREINE. I beg your pardon?

JUANA. I want six nights a week to write. I want access to a library, I wish to be part of a salon. I want a publication.

VICEREINE. Juana, don't be ridiculous. We are talking about marriage.

JUANA. Señora, as far as I'm concerned, marriage is the ridiculous part.

VICEREINE. You expect me to go to my uncle and—?

JUANA. Mi señora, you have been more than generous, and I expect nothing more from you. But those are my conditions.

VICEREINE. No man will agree to that!

JUANA. Which is why there is no man for me.

VICEREINE. You are impossible. You are selfish. Do not do this to me!

(Pause. JUANA grabs the VICEREINE's hands and respectfully bows her head.)

JUANA. Thank you for everything, Señora. I will never forget your kindness, your generosity, your affection. *(JUANA kisses the VICEREINE's cheek and pulls away.)*

VICEREINE. Juana...

JUANA. Xochitl, if you wouldn't mind helping me pack. I need to leave by morning.

XOCHITL. Si.

VICEREINE. You have no money!

JUANA. Xochitl, place these books on the bottom.

VICEREINE. You have no home!

JUANA. And these on top. I will read them on my way.

VICEREINE. There's nowhere for you to go.

JUANA. And with clothes, pack only what I brought.

VICEREINE. Juana! Xochitl! Stop! *(Beat.)* Two nights a week, no men in the salons, no publication.

JUANA. Five nights...a publication, men invited to the salon discussions every other week.

VICEREINE. Three nights, no men at the salon discussions, and no publication.

JUANA. Four nights, men at the salon once a month, full access to a library, and a thin publication.

VICEREINE. You learn too quickly. So be it.
JUANA. You agree?
VICEREINE. You have no excuse to say no.
XOCHITL *(whispers)*. Say no.
JUANA *(pause)*. Señora, please tell Don Fabio that it would be an honor for me to be his wife.
VICEREINE *(grabs her hands)*. Don't ever leave me again.

(There's a knock from the trunk and PEDRO, the VICE-ROY's valet, emerges.)

PEDRO. Good evening, my ladies.
XOCHITL. Don Pedro!
VICEREINE. Pedro, I don't remember saying you could enter.
PEDRO. I'm here at the Viceroy's discretion, mi señora. And he wishes for you to greet Father Nuñez.
VICEREINE. I'm in the middle of a lesson.
PEDRO. I'm sure the Viceroy would be happy to know that. But now he demands that you do differently.
VICEREINE *(pause)*. I see, well you can tell the Viceroy, tell him from me, that he and his demands—
PEDRO. Yes?
VICEREINE. Tell him that I will be there in a moment. *(Turns to JUANA.)* Congratulations, my dear. You have chosen wisely.
JUANA. Si, señora.
VICEREINE *(as PEDRO stares at JUANA)*. I will convince Don Fabio of the benefits of this particular arrangement. We will have the wedding as soon as possible. And Juana, from now on, we should refer to this Mayan—

XOCHITL. I'm Aztec!

VICEREINE. —This maid—by her given Christian name, Agnes. *(XOCHITL makes a face. PEDRO is still staring at JUANA.)* Come, Pedro, Padre Nuñez is waiting.

PEDRO. Si señora. *(VICEREINE and PEDRO exit.)*

JUANA *(trying to grasp)*. Xochitl, I just agreed to marry Don Fabio.

XOCHITL. Listen, *mi'jita*, I can stop the Vicereine right now and tell her you've decided against it.

JUANA. I used to be a poor girl on a poor farm. No one ever believed I would be able to get out. Now my poems are read in the great salons of the Viceroy's court. I have the Vicereine's favor. I left my family and past for this. All possibilities start and end here. So, if I must marry a dour man—

XOCHITL. You will find no poetry in his bed.

JUANA. Bodies are just clothes for our sexless and eternal souls. If they use my femaleness to trap me, I will use my femaleness to liberate me.

XOCHITL. The gods have provided you with a gift. They've chosen you to whisper in your ear. You should honor their gift... not sell it like a merchant.

JUANA. I'm not selling anything. *(Pause.)* I will write.

XOCHITL. But you will find no inspiration. A frog that wants to fly should not climb on a dodo's back. You have no affection for this man.

JUANA. Passion is for the primitive, Xochitl. You can't even write or read. You do not understand the decisions of the intellect.

XOCHITL. Then why do I know this decision is not sound?

Act I   THE SINS OF SOR JUANA

JUANA. Curb your instincts, Agnes. We are in world now. There are no spirits here. I will n   Fabio.

(A strong wind blows through the bedroom. XOCHITL is the only one that feels and hears it.)

SCENE FOUR

AT RISE: *VICEROY is sitting on his throne. A bound SILVIO is on his knees in front the VICEROY.*

VICEROY *(pulls out a paper)*. Silvio Burgas?
SILVIO. Yes.
VICEROY. Call me sir!
SILVIO. Yes, sir.
VICEROY. It says here that my guards caught you in one of my foyers, stealing.
SILVIO. It was a mistake... *(VICEROY looks at him.)* sir.
VICEROY. This is the fourth time we've been robbed. I have also heard that the Marqués de Laguna and the Duque de Granada were robbed. You wouldn't know anything about that? Would you?
SILVIO. Sir, you flatter me.
VICEROY. You unrepentant little bastard. I thought I'd seen the last of your sorry face when I left from Spain.
SILVIO. I came to find the riches of the Americas.
VICEROY. Well don't take them from me. If your father was still alive...
SILVIO. As far as I know, my father is still quite dead.

VICEROY. Which is what *you* should be. Silvio, you had an honorable father.

SILVIO. Who did nothing for me and my mother but pretend we didn't exist.

VICEROY. He had his *real* family to attend to. No whore can change that. And when your mother died, he did provide you with an education. Where is your gratitude?

SILVIO. Gratitude? I barely had anything to eat.

VICEROY. But you learned!

SILVIO. Knowledge does not make up for money.

VICEROY. There is no need to show you any mercy. Your father is dead. You are here and not in Spain. You are nothing but an ungrateful boy with no money and no title who has the nerve to steal from me.

(Enter PEDRO.)

PEDRO. Who's this?

VICEROY. This is Silvio Burgas, from Madrid, son of the Marqués de Salta.

PEDRO. Of the Marqués? Good evening, sir. *(Bows to SILVIO.)*

SILVIO. Better evening for you, I suppose.

VICEROY. No need for formality, Don Pedro. This is one of the Marqués' bastards.

PEDRO *(wrinkles his nose)*. Oh, I see. What did the little bastard do?

VICEROY. He's a thief. I'm trying to decide what to do about him. So what do you have to tell me. How is my dear wife? *(PEDRO whispers something in the VICEROY's ear.)* What??? *(The VICEROY stands and starts to pace.)*

PEDRO. Mi señor, I beg you, please calm down.

VICEROY. Calm down? You wish me to be calm?

PEDRO. I beseech you, señor. Be seated.

VICEROY. I issued that order to get rid of Juana! And now you are saying that...that...

PEDRO. She is now engaged to Don Fabio.

VICEROY. No! That Juana child is affecting my wife in the strangest ways. Oh, what is in the air of this odd new land? My constant wife is becoming defiant, distracted, disappearing before my very eyes. She's reading books behind locked doors; writing in hidden journals. Developing her thinking, she says. This cannot be good for her.

PEDRO. If it is any reassurance, señor, the Vicereine seems quite content.

VICEROY. And that is very troubling to me. I haven't seen her like this since the first year of our marriage. None of my actions seem to affect her anymore. Her mind is elsewhere. But she's mine, and I love her. I cannot lose Laura, you understand?

PEDRO. Well, perhaps the wedding shouldn't happen.

VICEROY. I cannot cancel another nobleman's wedding. *(Beat.)* Can I?

PEDRO. No, *(Pause.)* but perhaps you could encourage Don Fabio to cancel his own wedding.

VICEROY. The fool is so in love with Juana, he perspires at the very mention of her name. He thinks she is worth more than diamonds and gold. He would never cancel the proceeding.

PEDRO. He wouldn't *(Pause.)* unless Juana became less valuable. The girl is pure and untouched. But I could change that.

VICEROY. You flatter yourself; I know you have been spurned by the girl.

PEDRO. Sir! It is not my fault. I have used all my oft-victorious charms and she chooses to ignore me. And I'm not alone... I personally know that the finest men of this court have yelled, pleaded, cajoled, danced, pranced, bribed, lied, squirmed and primped to catch her eye. And yet she remains blind to us all.

VICEROY. She lives by reason and vows celibacy.

PEDRO. There is something faulty in her science.

SILVIO *(to himself)*. A good hunter never blames the game.

VICEROY. What did he say?

PEDRO. Nothing. Shut up, prisoner boy.

VICEROY. Tell me what you said.

SILVIO. You can't hunt a sparrow with a hammer or pull ocean fish without a net. The weapon must be tailored to the hunt.

PEDRO. I assure you, I have the finest of weapons.

SILVIO. Even a silver sword is worthless without a good soldier at the hilt.

PEDRO. Listen... you little...

SILVIO. And a good soldier knows the importance of strategy. Of surprise.

PEDRO. I have been trained for battle.

SILVIO. The object is to surprise but not to startle. The prey must be able to stare right at the predator and not even know she's the target... until it's too late.

VICEROY. Of course. *(Pause.)* That's it!! A man that Juana does not know or suspect.

SILVIO. A man with a different tactic than those practiced before. Perhaps a man with some education and yet...

VICEROY. Some shrewdness that contradicts his nobility!

Act I   THE SINS OF SOR JUANA   43

SILVIO. A man with all the trappings of nobility and wealth, yet none of the convictions. A man who has stolen all that he has earned. *(Pause.)* A thief of hearts.

VICEROY. Exactly! That's what I want. A thief of hearts.

SILVIO. Now... if I were a very wise and wealthy ruler... I would probably be thinking: Where can I hire this kind of man to seduce this Juana?

PEDRO. Hire? *(Exaggerated laugh.)*

SILVIO. Financial contracts are more binding than any favor.

VICEROY. Which is why I bought a guaranteed short stay in purgatory. I am not depending on Padre Nuñez for that favor.

SILVIO. All you need to do is employ a young, cultured, handsome scoundrel. *(PEDRO straightens his posture.)* Perhaps you have someone like that in the army? Or your court? Surely your court...

VICEROY. No, not in the army... not in my court...

SILVIO *(taunting PEDRO)*. The kitchen help? The stable boy?

VICEROY. No. *(Looking at SILVIO.)*

PEDRO *(beat)*. Señor, you certainly aren't considering...

VICEROY. Yes, I am...

PEDRO. Sir, he is not that handsome!

VICEROY. A vestal virgin's dream! And he's educated.

PEDRO. Sir, I have been in your faithful service for as long as I can remember.

VICEROY. So?

PEDRO. Every year you promise to give me an assignment of weight, a duty of challenge...

VICEROY. Dear impoverished and very distant cousin, is that ingratitude that I am hearing?

PEDRO. Señor...all I am asking is for an opportunity to exceed your low expectations.

VICEROY. Impress me with your silence. There are limits to someone like you. I want someone better. And if he's anything like his father, he has experience humiliating a woman.

SILVIO *(flattered)*. Your honor and my ruler, I am most taken aback...

PEDRO. Me too.

VICEROY. Silvio, do you think you can seduce a woman like Juana?

SILVIO. With all due, respect, SIR, there's nothing that makes me think I CAN'T.

(PEDRO snorts.)

VICEROY. You cocky little rooster. You know nothing about her.

SILVIO. More importantly, she knows nothing about me. I can be tailored to suit her needs. A rich, forgotten cousin? A dashing dancer? An expert bullfighter?

VICEROY. Nothing that blasé. Juana is quite unusual.

SILVIO. Ah! A religious and virtuous type?

VICEROY. Not exactly. *(Pause.)* She's strong. Very strong *(Points to his head.)* up here. Holds many facts in her head. Knows the answer before you've even asked the question. It was fascinating and entertaining, but now she has gone too far.

PEDRO. Señor, why are you doing this?

VICEROY. I want Laura to look at me again! I want Laura back from inside her mind. Silvio will help me!

PEDRO *(muttering)*. I cannot believe this!

SILVIO. Sir, I wish I could help...your dilemma really bears on my heart, but...

VICEROY. I will pay you one thousand reales! *(PEDRO reacts negatively without the VICEROY seeing him.)* I want Juana gone. You must seduce her...and have that information be as public and damning as possible. So much that Don Fabio cannot help but to repudiate her and my wife and I cannot help but to turn her away.

PEDRO. But he's a mess.

VICEROY. Pedro, attire this man and give him the tools with which to do his job. Let us just say that you are... are...

SILVIO. Don Silvio Granadera, Marqués de las Tampas. A progressive philosopher and a wealthy landowner, here on holiday in New Spain.

VICEROY. Soon, the Vicereine will be formally announcing the engagement of Don Fabio to Juana. I can think of no better place to introduce Don Silvio to the young girl. Pedro, unchain this man and lead him off to be bathed and dressed.

PEDRO *(beginning to unbind SILVIO, sees a necklace around SILVIO's neck).* But the cad is hiding stolen gold.

SILVIO. Hands off. It is mine. A gift from my mother.

VICEROY. Let him keep it. The chain will remind him of what is at stake. Remember, Silvio, if you succeed you will earn a good time, one thousand reales and your freedom. Should you fail, I suspect your future will be less bright. Now go! *(SILVIO exits.)* Pedro, keep an eye on him; we don't want him stealing anything other than Juana's honor. Prostitution is already in his blood, so I expect good results. Not a bad idea, eh?

PEDRO. A thousand reales to a stranger who steals? Forgive me, sir, but I would have been honored by your trust and not cost a coin.

VICEROY. You get what you pay for. I love my wife; she is the only one that matters. She is to know nothing of this financial arrangement. Ever.

PEDRO. Nothing.

(VICEREINE and JUANA walk in, arm in arm, talking. VICEREINE does not look at the VICEROY.)

VICEROY. Good evening.

JUANA. Good evening, dear sir. Don Pedro.

(The LADIES keep walking.)

VICEROY. Good evening, dear Laura.

VICEREINE. Forgive me, husband, my mind was elsewhere. You have heard the happy news? Juana is engaged to my uncle Fabio.

VICEROY. Pedro informed me... and I have already begun plans for the celebration. Perhaps we could discuss the details later tonight, alone.

VICEREINE. Señor, how kind, but as you know, these engagements are affairs between women. Besides, we both know that your evenings are quite full.

VICEROY. Never too full for you, *querida*.

VICEREINE. Señor, there's no need for you to trouble. Rest assured, all my needs are being well addressed. Good night, gentlemen. *(They exit.)*

VICEROY. I can rule an army but not my wife!

Act I THE SINS OF SOR JUANA 47

PEDRO. I am certain the Vicereine would be impressed by the costs you bear for her.

VICEROY. Everything may have a price, but not everyone has to pay. When Silvio does tarnish Juana's name, Don Fabio is bound to avenge her. And then, we will be rid of the thief as well. *(Pause.)* Ingenious, eh.

PEDRO. Ingenious, sir.

VICEROY. Never doubt the Viceroy.

PEDRO. Never, sir.

VICEROY. Lord, forgive me, I have no other choice.

PEDRO. No other, sir.

VICEROY. This is all for Laura.

PEDRO. For the nobility of love, sir.

VICEROY *(pause)*. Shut up, Pedro.

PEDRO. Yes, sir.

SCENE FIVE

AT RISE: *Convent. SOR SARA is holding a tray of food outside JUANA's door. Inside the room, JUANA is half-dressed, in knickers, preparing for her engagement party at the court.*

SARA *(knocking)*. Sor Juana, dear Christian Sister, it is Sor Sara. Open the door. *(No response.)* Sor Filothea sent me with food. Be so gracious as to open. *(No response.)* You should open. You could eat. We could be friends. *(Pause.)* I take no pleasure in standing here, talking to a door. If it were up to me, I would let you be hungry. Direct a word this way. *(Pause.)* Or does the devil have your tongue? *(Pause.)* We burned your books this morning. *(JUANA reacts.)* They made a nice fire, but short lived. Paper turns to smoke much quicker than timber. *(Pause.)* Do you repent, Sor Juana? *(Pause.)* ARE YOU REPENTING?

JUANA. NO. I AM NOT REPENTING.

SARA. God, He knows what you are doing in there! *(SARA places the tray on the floor exits.)*

(We are in JUANA's room in the court. JUANA is young and excited, she runs up to XOCHITL.)

JUANA. Xochitl, I just created the best lines...

XOCHITL. Hush, *mi'jita*. Your engagement party is moments away and look at you. Did you write a poem for Don Fabio?

JUANA. That thing? *(Shows it to her.)* It's done.

XOCHITL. Then sit down...I must do something with your hair.

JUANA. But...

XOCHITL. And eat something! You need some food. *(Begins to go to the door.)*

JUANA. But there will be food at the celebration.

XOCHITL. Which you are not to touch. "It is unbecoming for a fine lady to eat and speak at the same time." The Vicereine's order.

JUANA. So listen to this!

XOCHITL. Juana!

JUANA *(clears her throat. Exuberant).*
    Reason is a sword,
    With purpose on both sides

Act I   THE SINS OF SOR JUANA   49

> The base to defend
> The point to make others die.
>
> If, conscious of the danger,
> I negotiate the blade
> Blame not the witless sword
> For the bloody choice I made.

XOCHITL *(beat)*. Don Fabio will not like that one.

JUANA. Don Fabio cannot dislike what he does not see. What do you think?

XOCHITL. You know exactly what I think, my child. But you have made up your mind and now you must get ready.

JUANA. But I have more...

XOCHITL. I know...so much more. But it does not matter to them...especially if you are going to be late to your own engagement party.

JUANA. But I have to get this all down...

XOCHITL. Juana, you have made a choice; you now have duties.

JUANA. But thoughts are rushing in...ideas, images. Don't you understand?

XOCHITL. I understand more than you will ever know.

VICEREINE *(offstage)*. Juana. Juana Inés!

JUANA *(begins to crawl under her bed)*. Tell her you do not know where I am.

XOCHITL. Look at you! Postponing your engagement for a poem!

JUANA. It will only be a moment. I promise. I just need to...

VICEREINE. Juana?

(VICEREINE opens the door. JUANA lets the dust ruffle fall. XOCHITL turns to face VICEREINE.)

VICEREINE. Where is that girl?
XOCHITL. Mi Doña, I'm certain she's not far from here.
VICEREINE. We are all waiting for her. Did she do as I asked and write a poem in honor of Don Fabio?
XOCHITL. Yes, mi Doña.
VICEREINE. As long as all her poems are about her husband's virtues... Don Fabio will allow her to write, recite, and certainly publish.
XOCHITL. I think she is practicing her very *short* ode as we speak.
VICEREINE. Let us go find her. The time to perform is now.

(VICEREINE rushes back out, XOCHITL picks up the tray, follows her and looks around the room before closing the door behind her. JUANA begins to crawl out from under her bed but hears someone open the door and she goes back into hiding. SILVIO sneaks into the room and quietly closes the door behind him. He is obviously looking for information on JUANA. He stops at her writings. He picks them up.)

SILVIO. "A poem for Don Fabio." Let's see... Blah-Blah-Blah.

(An offended JUANA hits her head on the bed. SILVIO begins to look at the bed. A noise at the door. SILVIO rushes to hide in the closet and slams the door. JUANA

Act I   THE SINS OF SOR JUANA   51

thinks he exited the room. PEDRO opens the door to JUANA's room.)

PEDRO. Juana, the Viceroy commands that you... *(Noticing she is not in the room, he does not close the door.)* Where is the little...? *(Sniffs.)* Ah, but it still carries her scent. *(To an imaginary JUANA.)* Ah, it appears we are alone, little Juana. *(PEDRO walks around the room. He eyes the bed and walks toward it.)* Where are you, Juanita? *(He pauses and sits on the bed.)* Is this the bed where you lie, little Juanita? *(He grabs a pillow and talks to it.)* Is this where you dream, your woman dreams? *(He hugs the pillow tenderly.)* Is this where your heart trembles with anticipation of...of... *(Listens to the pillow, with disgust.)* a book? How many times have you met my gaze and dismissed me by simply turning the page? WHY? You can love me, want me, fear me. But do not dismiss me! I too have a heart and mind...and I hate being so alone. *(Tenderly.)* Are you listening to me? *(Beat.)* I said, are you listening to me? Take this poetry, you wench.

(PEDRO jams and rubs the pillow onto his crotch. XOCHITL appears at the doorway.)

XOCHITL. Señor!
PEDRO *(stops shocked)*. Xochitl!
PEDRO & XOCHITL *(in unison)*. What are you doing here?
XOCHITL *(curtsies but is outraged)*. Señor, this is Juana's room.
PEDRO. It is?
XOCHITL. And that is Juana's bed!

PEDRO *(changing strategy).* I know. And thank God you are here, for I've suffered a terrible accident. In my search for Juana, I have fallen.

XOCHITL. It certainly seems that way.

PEDRO. I carelessly tripped. And I have injured myself so badly, that I had to drag myself to this position.

XOCHITL. It is quite a position.

PEDRO. I fear I cannot walk.

XOCHITL. You are in pain?

PEDRO. I am sore.

XOCHITL. I see.

PEDRO. And now, you must help me.

XOCHITL. Señor, I will do what I can.

(XOCHITL does not move. PEDRO realizes this and must crawl to XOCHITL and pull himself up. PEDRO uses XOCHITL as a crutch.)

PEDRO. Do not mention this incident to the Vicereine. I do not wish for her to worry about my health. *(XOCHITL grunts and sighs.)* Am I too heavy?

XOCHITL. No, señor. *(Grunts.)* My shoulders are used to this type of burden.

PEDRO. You Mayans are so strong.

XOCHITL *(jams the pillow in his mouth).* Bite this, señor; it will muffle the agony.

(Exeunt. Pause. JUANA begins to crawl out from under the bed.)

JUANA. That insolent little...

Act I   THE SINS OF SOR JUANA   53

(SILVIO opens the door to the closet. JUANA, in a crawling position, and SILVIO look at each other in shock.)

SILVIO. I'm sorry. *(Beat.)* I beg your pardon. *(SILVIO shuts himself in the closet. JUANA is stunned. She stands up, covers herself with a shawl, and opens the closet door. A warm light from the closet; SILVIO bows. There is an immediate tension and attraction between the two.)* Don Silvio Granadera, Marqués de las Tampas. Master of Letters and Philosophy. *(Beat.)* May I? *(He steps out of the closet.)*

JUANA. Are you looking for a dress?

SILVIO. I am looking for Juana Inés Ramirez de Asbaje.

JUANA. In there? No. No. No. She's much too complicated to fit in such a small space. *(She pulls out a dress.)* Here, try the blue one.

SILVIO. I beg your pardon?

JUANA. Sir, you are a gentleman. Surely you know that it is highly improper for a gentleman to speak alone in a young woman's bedroom. You are either here to steal from me or borrow clothes.

SILVIO. I prefer the red one. It's in the back.

JUANA. It is a favorite of mine as well. *(She hands him the red dress.)* I hope it fits. On your way out, please shut the door. *(SILVIO starts to pull off his shirt.)* Señor, what are you doing?

SILVIO. I am changing.

JUANA. Here?

SILVIO. Certainly, what if I should return to my room and the dress should not fit?

JUANA. Señor, surely you do not intend to... SEÑOR!

SILVIO *(pulls on the skirt)*. If these are the trappings I must wear to allow my soul to speak to yours, so be it. What do you think?

JUANA. Lovely.

SILVIO. This is rather uncomfortable. How can you stand wearing something this tight every day?

JUANA. Tight? You are not even wearing the bustier.

SILVIO. Should I?

JUANA. If you wish to be dressed correctly, yes. *(Hands SILVIO the bustier.)*

SILVIO. I see. *(Takes off the shirt.)*

JUANA. Señor!

SILVIO. Really, Señorita Juana, I'm surprised by your surprise. Aren't you the one that wrote "Souls are sexless"?

JUANA. Sir, you are not exposing your soul.

SILVIO. Unless this is too much for you.

JUANA. Allow me.

(JUANA puts on SILVIO's coat to cover herself and helps SILVIO with the bustier. She is now dressed as a man, he as a woman.)

SILVIO. Thank you, señorita, I appreciate your cooperation. And I simply don't want people to speak ill of me at the party. You know how society events are. So many tedious rules. Somebody would be sure to comment on the impropriety of my lack of bustier. *(Gasps.)* Delicately. Delicately. Santa Madre de Jesus (Holy Mother of Jesus), how do you breathe with these on?

JUANA. We are not supposed to. Don't you know, we spend our whole lives holding our breath and our tongue. *(Beat.)* Why are you here?

Act I THE SINS OF SOR JUANA

SILVIO. I am here to meet you.

JUANA. I'm impressed. A man that dares dress like a woman to meet a woman must be quite a man.

SILVIO. I hear you are quite a woman

JUANA. It depends on what "quite a woman" is.

SILVIO. I also heard you were beautiful.

JUANA. And now you can see if you heard correctly.

SILVIO. There are certain men that say there are only so many virtues a woman can shoulder.

JUANA. And then there is you.

SILVIO. There is always an exception for the exceptional. And you, *querida*, are wise in noting it.

JUANA. Oh, you fancy yourself different from other men?

SILVIO. No. It is quite plain; I am different.

JUANA. Underneath it all, you still look like other men. You walk like other men. Your scent is like others.

SILVIO *(sexy)*. But I can assure you, my dear, my taste is quite different. *(Pause. Sees a book on the desk.)* Ah, the clever girl reads. *Don Quixote*...Cervantes...quite the master...pursuit of windmills.

JUANA. A wonderful book. "It is a mark of well-born men to show gratitude for benefits received and ingratitude..." *(Overlapping with SILVIO.)*

SILVIO. "...and ingratitude is one of the sins which most offends God."

JUANA. You know the quote.

SILVIO. I know the book.

JUANA. "The reason for the unreason with which you treat my reason so weakens..." *(Overlapping with SILVIO.)*

SILVIO. "...so weakens my reason, that with reason, I complain of your beauty."

JUANA. Impressive.

SILVIO. Hardly. I had a lonely childhood; except I read. Is the story the same for you?

JUANA. Yes.

SILVIO. Curse or blessing this passion of the intellect?

JUANA. It is both *(Beat.)* and it is neither. For every passion in every intellect is different.

SILVIO. And yet the soul's search is the same, is it not?

JUANA. The search for Understanding?

SILVIO. The search for Union.

JUANA. Why are you here?

SILVIO *(long pause)*. Let us not play games, Señorita Juana. This is America! *(Tries to remove bustier.)* Spain suffocates me and I refuse to be a wealthy man with bankrupt inspiration. I am ready for true challenge, to set roots in a land that will judge all of us on the nobility of our actions, not our ancestry. *(Unties skirt.)* I am here to build a life based on the merits of my ideas, the tenacity of my spirit and the strength of my body. *(Pause.)* You, on the other hand, are to wed Don Fabio.

JUANA. Yes.

SILVIO *(puts on his regular clothes)*. I wish you much happiness.

JUANA. Thank you.

SILVIO. The Viceroy said it will be a beautiful betrothal.

JUANA. Don Fabio is the Vicereine's uncle.

SILVIO. A splendid match. Don Fabio is a great gentleman...

JUANA. Yes.

SILVIO. Very decent, but very dull.

JUANA. He is the noble man who will be my husband.

SILVIO. The man you love?

JUANA. The man I will marry.

SILVIO. You penned this poem for him?

JUANA. Your thoughts, señor?

SILVIO *(smiles. Looks down at the poem. Smiles again)*. One word only can express what I think.

JUANA. Yes?

SILVIO *(pause)*. Rewrite.

JUANA. Pardon?

SILVIO. The poem is bland and uninspired.

JUANA. Señor!

SILVIO. I can speak plainly, on equal terms, or I can coddle you with vapid politeness; which do you prefer?

JUANA *(beat)*. The truth.

SILVIO. "Love's delicacy consists of being loved." Although I am impressed by the quickness of your mind; your poetic passion is in stupor.

JUANA. You surprised me. This is not my best work.

SILVIO. And why is it not? Excuses. That is what they all say. They hand you something and say "This is not my best work."

JUANA. Señor, I handed you nothing.

SILVIO. I cannot believe I came from Madrid for this!

JUANA. You were sent from Madrid?

SILVIO. The words are elegant, but there is no life, no blood, no spirit. I cannot publish this!!!

JUANA. Publish? Publish my work?

SILVIO. Our printing press cannot run this. It just goes to prove, intelligence does not equal artistry. There is no art here.

JUANA. Sir, your rudeness and shortsightedness are dwarfed only by your unfounded arrogance.

SILVIO. I beg your pardon?

JUANA. The truth is: I do write poetry and I write it well.

SILVIO. I know I should be gallant and accept your claim with grace.

JUANA. I hope instead you challenge my words to a poetic race.

SILVIO. You challenge me to challenge you. Very well, I will oblige. Juana Inés, be so kind and clever as to create a poem, now.

JUANA. A poem. Any subject? Topic?

SILVIO. A love poem. *(Pause.)* A love poem...dedicated to me.

JUANA. Surely you are aware of the impropriety; I am a promised woman!

SILVIO. And deeply inspired by your beloved, I know. But this is not a test of your ability to love, but of your ability to write. Are you creative and brave enough to write a poem about adoring me?

JUANA *(pause. She thinks. Slowly but with confidence).*
"Silvio, that I could place my love on you
Is a truth I must decree
To Love a Man as Vile as few
Confirms sin's weight and gravity

Dearly, I wish, when my eyes fall on you
That I could deny a love so base and low
But Reason's force so hard and true
Demands I admit the sin I know

For the Crime of loving you, there is no pardon
Save to confess and have my heart harden."

(Long pause.)

Act I THE SINS OF SOR JUANA 59

SILVIO. Do you cross-stitch?

JUANA. No.

SILVIO. Forget writing; learn to cross-stitch. It will make your life much easier.

JUANA. You found the poem so inadequate?

SILVIO. Señorita Juana, I do not know how much exposure a girl like you has had and since I do not wish to agitate such a tender young lady as yourself, I shall stay silent.

JUANA. Your hard words will not break me.

SILVIO *(pause)*. All right then...

> I'd take pride to watch you recite, to a court of worldly men.
> I would disperse worldwide your verse and venerate your pen.
> In our lively, lovely house, the library would be yours
> The summers would consist of faraway exotic tours.
> Perhaps I stand alone but I find it quite a bore
> For others to force a talent to make her life a chore.
> Instead, my dear, I implore you to Accept my pure romance
> By the sun write plays, in the moonlight, with me, dance.
>
> All could be yours, All could be mine
> If we had just met— Different place, different time.

JUANA *(pause)*.

> Your views, Don Silvio,
>   are different: rich, sublime
> But voicing them here
>   could be a serious crime.

SILVIO.
>Risks must be made...
>To improve each other's life
>I'll be your loving editor
>If you'll be my passionate wife.

JUANA. A moment ago you roared I was a woman with no art.

SILVIO.
>You are divinity. You are trinity
>True mind, true soul, true heart.

(Long pause. SILVIO and JUANA stand perfectly still. No kiss. No leaning to kiss. Just still desire. Outside the door, the NOVICE picks up the uneaten tray of food.)

NOVICE. Sor Juana, you must let something touch your lips. *(Exits.)*
JUANA. I must go.
SILVIO. Hurry. Don Fabio, the Decent, is waiting.
JUANA *(biting)*. Good night and good-bye, Don Silvio Granadera, Marqués de las Tampas. I enjoyed your little refrain. I now have larger matters to attend to. Enjoy your trip back to Spain. *(She starts to exit.)*
SILVIO. Señorita Juana?
JUANA. Yes?
SILVIO *(teasing)*. Dedicate your first cross-stitch to me.

(JUANA slams the door. It echoes.)

INTERMISSION

ACT TWO

SCENE ONE

SETTING: *The convent.*

AT RISE: *The NOVICE wanders in and begins arranging the altar. Underneath a cloth, she discovers a book that has not been burned. She is alarmed, stands and is about to turn it in. She stops, opens it. She hears men's voices, slams the book, hides it and scoots away. The MEN enter. We are in the court. VICEROY discussing matters with PEDRO. SILVIO is apart, reading.*

PEDRO. Mi señor, the Vicereine has made a list of requests for Don Fabio's wedding to Juana Inés.
VICEROY. I'm sure she has. What does the Vicereine list?
PEDRO *(unrolls a large piece of paper)*. Various things. Guests, food, flowers, the normal.
VICEROY. What is her estimate?
PEDRO. Five-hundred reales.
VICEROY. Five-hundred reales?
PEDRO. Yes, it's more economical to wed Juana off than to hire the bastard.
VICEROY. Silvio, did you hear that? My valet says you are bad business.
SILVIO. I think your valet is still a little sore.
PEDRO. Listen, you little...

61

VICEROY. Boys. Boys. Enough. Silvio, you've had several days. How have things advanced with the girl?

SILVIO. Matters are where they should be. I have planted the seed.

PEDRO. What? So soon? But how is that possible... I've...

SILVIO. In her mind. Thoughts are taking root.

PEDRO. No! No time for thoughts. Attack from all sides. Allow her to think there's no other way but yours. Wear down all defense. Exhaust her, confuse her, overpower. Sir, I am now very concerned about this project.

VICEROY. I can see the concern etched in your face.

PEDRO. A thousand reales for this?

VICEROY. All I know is that your life and fortune depend on you doing things correctly, Silvio.

(JUANA enters. SILVIO, PEDRO and VICEROY stop. JUANA bows.)

JUANA. Good morning, dear sir and noble gentlemen. *(Pause.)* Pardon me? Am I interrupting something?

VICEROY. No. No! A ray of sunshine and inspiration. *(Goes to JUANA and takes her hands.)* How are you today?

JUANA. Grateful for all your efforts. Thank you for the lovely engagement celebration.

VICEROY. Don Fabio is a lucky man.

JUANA. No, I am a lucky woman, having protectors as yourself to guide me.

VICEROY. Yes, well. If you are looking for the Vicereine, I believe the dear woman is in her chamber.

JUANA. I came to direct a kind word to your guest.

VICEROY. Guest?

JUANA. The Marqués. Don Silvio.

(PEDRO and SILVIO look at each other.)

VICEROY *(arm around JUANA; in a whisper).* A fine young man from one of the best families in Valencia.
SILVIO. Good morning, Señorita Juana Inés.
JUANA. Good morning, Don Silvio. Good morning, Don Pedro.

(PEDRO mumbles embarrassed.)

VICEROY. Don Silvio, it appears that this young lady wishes to speak to you.
SILVIO. What an honor.
JUANA. Oh, it's nothing really. I have something for Don Silvio.

(THE VICEREINE bursts in.)

VICEREINE. Juana, there you are!
JUANA. Mi Señora, I was just telling the Viceroy how pleased you were with the engagement celebration.
VICEREINE. Oh yes, husband, you are splendid. Juana, you must come with me immediately; I need to speak with you, alone.
JUANA. I'm sorry, *mi señora*, I cannot. *(Long silence.)* I have just requested a moment with Don Silvio.
VICEREINE. Don Silvio?
VICEROY. Our guest.
SILVIO. *Encantado, mi señora.*

VICEREINE. I see. *(Pause.)* Fine, as long as you don't forget to honor all your commitments. I'll await you in my chamber. Do not take long. Good day, gentlemen. *(VICEREINE begins to exit.)*

VICEROY. Laura, Pedro and I were on our way to meet Padre Nuñez.

PEDRO. What?

VICEROY. I think you should join us.

VICEREINE. Now? I'm terribly busy.

VICEROY. Too busy for your lord? Come now, Laura. Confession is good for the soul. *(Takes VICEREINE's arm.)* Let's go, Pedro.

PEDRO. But Padre Nuñez...

VICEROY. Is waiting.

PEDRO. Yes, sir. *(VICEROY and VICEREINE exit.)* Juana, beware, none of us is what we seem. *(PEDRO exits.)*

SILVIO. Strange man.

JUANA. Did I perturb them?

SILVIO. I'm afraid you perturb us all. *(Beat.)* I am surprised and honored that you are suddenly directing a word my way. A week has passed and you have not even met my gaze.

JUANA. Don Silvio, I'm afraid that I owe you an apology.

SILVIO. But if I offended you...

JUANA. Señor, I must admit... The eve we met, I found your comments disturbing... even painful. And I became very angry at you.

SILVIO. For speaking the truth?

JUANA. For giving me hope. *(Pause.)* Your candor, Don Silvio, is the most gracious gift I have ever received. It made me think... it made me... feel. You appear to have both knowledge and experience.

SILVIO. My family has lived for centuries in the cultured city of Salamanca. The university has been my playground. *(Beat.)* I like to consider myself a professor and tutor in many things.

JUANA *(beat)*. And so I approach with a humble question. I have always been alone when... But perhaps you... Are you able... are you willing... to possibly teach... a woman?

SILVIO. Depends on what the woman would like to learn.

JUANA. Señor, nothing less than the ways of the world.

SILVIO. Really?

JUANA. I am ready for everything. Don't be gentle. *(She hands him some poems.)* Criticize me. Help me improve. Show me the rules of the literary world. Go on... read them.

SILVIO *(tries to pull himself together)*. Hm. This one is charming although the syntax is a little awkward.

JUANA. Exactly! I thought so as well. And yet...

SILVIO.
> "My body answers yours, magnet to metal
> But I am not your prize
> Boast not of your conquest
> Reject me
> Slip away from my arms, my breasts
> You are still a prisoner
> In my poem."

(Beat.)

JUANA. Too much?
SILVIO. Sometimes discomfort is completely appropriate.
JUANA. Yes.

SILVIO.
> "You've undressed my heart, dissolved it
> Your hands drowning in its liquid"

(Beat.) I would suggest a different word here than "drowning."

JUANA. But that is the precise word.

SILVIO. Vagueness has its virtues.

JUANA. If I wasn't a lady and you weren't a gentleman, and you were forced to speak your honest mind, with no rules, no avoidance of cruelty. *(Places her hand firmly on his lower arm.)* What would you say of the works before you?

SILVIO *(pause; honest)*. I would say that they are by no means perfect...the meter dances to a strange beat, the rhyme is sometimes forced, and the length on some is... But they are eloquent and ferocious...betraying a wisdom too ripe for your young years. I would say that whatever you do, you must keep writing. Imperfect poems are the only ones that make a significant impact on the soul. *(JUANA kisses the inside of SILVIO's hand.)* Juana?

JUANA. Please do not tell the Vicereine or Don Fabio about my behavior. I assure you, I am usually a virtuous, controlled woman.

SILVIO. What a pity.

JUANA. Don Silvio, I have not been able to sleep since the eve we met. I close my eyes and I see you. You are caught between my heart and my voice, trapped inside my eyelids at night. Nothing is right: My blood is thinking and my mind is feeling; I'm going mad...and you are making me this way.

SILVIO. But you are to wed another man.

JUANA. Yes! And my reason judged that as the most intelligent, prudent choice to make.

SILVIO. A very sound decision indeed. It ensures your safety and maintenance for the rest of your days. Juana, rest assured that this "impulse" towards me could be nothing more than a whim, a sweet fancy, a craving of some sort...

JUANA. Please stop pretending!

SILVIO. Pretending?

JUANA. You are not like the others who pass through these halls. Don't be so polite, so reasonable, so proper. I know what you want.

SILVIO. What do I want?

JUANA *(pause)*. Everything. You dare hope for everything. It's in your eyes, Don Silvio. *(Beat.)* Why did you come here? My life was decided and clear. I had no pangs. I don't want any man. I don't want any marriage. Ever! And yet, I want you. Why?

SILVIO. I could leave.

JUANA. Yes, but I'm afraid you *(Touches her head.)* will not go away. You spoke words I had thought but had never said out loud.

SILVIO. Words are syllables and air.

JUANA. You said, in your world, a woman would have access to the world. Is that true?

SILVIO *(pause)*. I stand by my name.

JUANA. And she would be allowed—no, encouraged—to write, to read, to partake in social intellectual functions? Allowed to shine without compromise or fear? To speak her mind and her heart as loudly as she pleased? And in spite of what others said, you would honor and protect this freedom ... *her* freedom?

SILVIO. I stand by my name.

JUANA. And you would love her, love her without trying to change her?

SILVIO. I would love *you*, Juana. *(Beat.)* Are these the reasons you seek me out?

JUANA. Honestly, señor, for the first time in my life I am not reaching my decision by reason ... but trying to reason my impulse. It defies logic. I am going backwards ... and I know not whether to celebrate freedom or weep defeat.

SILVIO. Can I sway you to rejoice?

JUANA. Only if you tell me that you speak the truth?

SILVIO *(pause)*. I stand by my name.

JUANA. I want to believe you.

SILVIO. And I you. How do I know your feelings are true?

JUANA. I assure you, señor, they are.

SILVIO. And if you abandon me like you have Don Fabio?

JUANA. Abandoning you would be like abandoning the best within myself, allowing the rot and moss at the corners of my spirit to move to the center of my being. Don Silvio, abandoning you would be forsaking a gift that God, in all his grace, has given.

SILVIO *(pause; SILVIO is touched, yet)*. Words. You writers think words are always the answer.

JUANA. What else can I give you, but what I do best?

SILVIO. Dear Juana, a loving, caring, soulful and ... *tangible* gesture will do more than any poem.

JUANA *(pause)*. Monday night, I shall be alone. Meet me then. I will demonstrate the depth of my commitment.

SILVIO. I shall be there. So...do you love me, Juana?
JUANA. I think I do. I dream I do. I feel I do. *(Walks away.)* But Silvio, I have no name to stand by...

(JUANA exits. SILVIO looks after her. PEDRO emerges; clapping his hands.)

PEDRO. Nice work. Very nice work. Despite my efforts. Amazing how the illegitimate can find each other and beget more illegitimacy.
SILVIO. Don Pedro, with all due respect, bite your tongue before I pummel your face into the dirt.
PEDRO. Testy. Testy. Remember, Silvio, you are supposed to get into her *(Makes vulgar movement.)* before she gets into you. *(Taps his heart.)*
SILVIO *(pause)*. You know what I like about being a bastard, Don Pedro?
PEDRO. No, Silvio, do tell.

(SILVIO grabs PEDRO and gives him a loud, boisterous kiss, then throws him roughly to the floor.)

SILVIO. Our ability to love and forgive.

(SILVIO exits. PEDRO gets up, furious.)

SCENE TWO

AT RISE: *The convent. SOR FILOTHEA is outside JUANA's door. She's bearing a jug of water. A nightmare.*

FILOTHEA *(knocks)*. Sor Juana, can you hear me? I am concerned. You have not eaten in five days.

(The VICEREINE enters and caresses JUANA on the bed.)

VICEREINE. You look weary and pale.
JUANA. Madre Filothea?
FILOTHEA. You are wasting food, Sor Juana.
JUANA *(sees the VICEREINE)*. I have had no appetite.
FILOTHEA. It is a sin to deny the gifts God brings.
JUANA & VICEREINE *(pointed)*. I know.
FILOTHEA. We miss you, Juana. Can you not open the door? Join us again? Eat! *(Beat.)* Are you ill?
JUANA. Yes. Hungry. Sick.

(VICEROY comes out from closet or underneath the bed and grabs the VICEREINE. NOVICE wanders into the room. PEDRO comes out of the trunk. Fever. The VICEREINE feels JUANA's forehead.)

VICEREINE. You're burning.
JUANA. Did YOU burn my books, Filothea?
FILOTHEA. Don't you understand? It was an act of love.

(VICEROY passionately kisses VICEREINE.)

JUANA. Understand love?

Act II   THE SINS OF SOR JUANA   71

FILOTHEA. Beware, Juana, of the strangeness of solitude.
JUANA. I'm afraid. I'm not alone.
FILOTHEA. You're not alone. Be not afraid, Juana, undo what you have done.
JUANA. Is that possible?

(VICEREINE pulls away from the VICEROY and goes to JUANA.)

FILOTHEA *(beat)*. Sor Juana, from now on, I am to leave nothing but a jug of water at your door... until you pull out every thread from your cross-stitch.

(The VICEROY circles the bed.)

NOVICE & JUANA. The cross-stitch.
FILOTHEA. Will you not open the door?

(VICEREINE, PEDRO, VICEROY are all holding JUANA from the door.)

JUANA. I can't!

(All DREAM CHARACTERS exit.)

FILOTHEA. God help you, my friend. *(Exits.)*

(SILVIO enters. He and JUANA look at each other.)

SILVIO. If others find out...
JUANA. There will be consequences...
SILVIO. For you.

JUANA. For us both.

SILVIO *(pause)*. I was thinking about the poem you gave me... It keeps running through my mind.

JUANA. Yes?

SILVIO. I now believe that "drowning" is the precise word. *(Beat.)* This is dangerous.

JUANA. I am a promised woman.

SILVIO. More importantly, you are a woman of promise. And I will not compromise your future.

JUANA. We are that future.

SILVIO. I wish that was true.

JUANA. It is true. Do not leave. *(Pause.)* I have something to give you.

SILVIO. A poem?

JUANA. Something more... personal... tangible. *(She begins to unhook the front of her dress.)*

SILVIO. Juana...

JUANA. Don Silvio, it took all my resolve to reach this decision. I do not care to back down now. *(Continues to unhook the front of her dress.)*

SILVIO. Juana...

JUANA. Do you want me to stop?

SILVIO. Yes. *(She does. Pause.)* No.

JUANA. Well? *(He reaches for her. JUANA takes SILVIO's hand and places his palm against her stomach and guides it up her body, to her breasts. They embrace. She pulls a cloth from her cleavage and gently pushes him away. She hands him the cloth.)* This is what I wanted to give you.

SILVIO. A cross-stitching?

JUANA. It's one of the most difficult things I've ever done. Did I capture it correctly? Your family crest.

Act II   THE SINS OF SOR JUANA   73

SILVIO. Oh! Now I see it. Of course. The crest.
JUANA. Yes, you see. That's a lion.
SILVIO. Yes.
JUANA. For courage, I suppose.
SILVIO. Yes, and the book for learning. The ship for adventure and... what is that?
JUANA. Oh, that. I beg your pardon. That's blood.
SILVIO. Very real.
JUANA. I'm afraid so. *(Shows him her finger.)* I pricked myself.
SILVIO. Badly?
JUANA. It will heal. Pain is part of the process, no?
SILVIO. Unfortunately.
JUANA. And then there's the last design.
SILVIO. The candle.
JUANA. What does the candle stand for?
SILVIO. Many things really. Enlightenment.
JUANA. Ah, the truth?
SILVIO. Why yes. The truth.
JUANA. Interesting... especially in light that you are lying to me.
SILVIO. Sorry?
JUANA. Don Silvio, this is not the Tampas family crest. Either you aren't very familiar with your lineage... or you are not who you claim to be.
SILVIO. I beg your pardon?
JUANA. Yes, you should. A publisher? From Salamanca? Madrid? Valencia? Where exactly has your family lived for the last century?
SILVIO. Juana, you are confused.
JUANA. Confused, yes. Wrong, no. This crest is a product of imagination. As is, perhaps your name.

SILVIO. You don't know what you are saying.

JUANA. I wanted to make something just for you... cross-stitch your family crest. But I did some reading. I discovered there is no you. There is no Tampas family. The contradictions made sense. All I could think is why? WHY? Why is this wonderful learned man lying, using a false identity? What profit is there in imitating a nobleman?

SILVIO. I believe this conversation needs to...

JUANA. And then suddenly I knew! I knew! I understood!

SILVIO. There is nothing to understand.

JUANA *(beat)*. Misbegotten. Illegitimate. Unwanted. *(Beat.)* A bastard.

SILVIO. I have never been so insulted!

JUANA. I find that hard to believe.

SILVIO. I am not a common, wreck of a child like... like...

JUANA. Like me? *(Pause.)* Marked at conception... asking forgiveness for sins that were not ours. Judged by station and birth more than merit. Kept at bay by others' low expectations. Guilty until proven innocent. And if I do anything right, I am treated as a carnival curiosity... and waved about like a banner. *(Pause.)* That's who I am. Who are you?

SILVIO. Silvio Burgas, bastard son of The Marqués de Gorgóna...

JUANA. Why did you not tell me earlier?

SILVIO. And court your disdain?

JUANA. Silvio, you do not understand me.

SILVIO. My mother, my father, and I all cursed the day I was born. Why should you be different?

JUANA. Surely you did not think that...

SILVIO. You have discovered my reality. I am but a common man of noble roots. *(Pause. Sincere.)* Juana, I am sorry. *(Begins to exit.)*

JUANA. When I was twelve, I cut my hair, donned boy's clothing and for a brief moment enjoyed a new dimension of possibility. *(SILVIO stops and faces her.)* I was disguised but more myself than I'd ever been. Perhaps masks give the freedom to reveal our deeper truths... to reach the point where lies are no longer necessary.

SILVIO. The lies are no longer necessary.

JUANA. And I know all the truths about you?

SILVIO *(pause)*. Juana, do not have any illusions. I am a misbegotten...

JUANA. Bastard son... but hardly common. We must leave while we can.

SILVIO. And go where? I have no name, no wealth, no social gentility...

JUANA. Don Silvio, I know the value of gold, the worth of noble birth, the price of power. I have read books on faraway lands, and written poetry from my heart. But, señor, I never dreamed that a man would open so many doors within my soul and that his eyes could become windows to a bright future. Sir, if you search for wealth, seek no further than yourself.

SILVIO. Juana, luxury and comfort are not to be disdained.

JUANA. No. It is a pleasure to *live* with them, and a tragedy to live *for* them. I nearly threw away my life for the comfort of living here.

SILVIO. If words were gold...

JUANA. They will be. We will earn others' respect, by truly valuing the wealth we possess. The worthiness of our wit, our minds, our words, will open doors. This is a new

land; and good things grow from a love that is worthy
and true. I promise, as you enrich me, I will enrich you.

SILVIO *(pause, removes his chain and places it around
JUANA's neck).*
    My mother worked her wretched life
    She gave me this gold chain
    It protected me for twenty years
    It is my only worldly gain
    All I have and all I am, is yours.

JUANA.
    And since the soul is the body's life
    I will breathe your air, and be your wife.
    Let us leave tonight, in secret.
(They kiss.)

SILVIO. I'll await you past midnight at the twisted oak that divides the stream. I will not leave without you.

(Suddenly PEDRO and the VICEREINE enter.)

PEDRO. Here they are!
VICEREINE. What are you doing alone with this man?

(SILVIO pushes PEDRO out of the way and runs.)

JUANA. Go!
PEDRO. I told you, señora!
VICEREINE. Get him, you fool. Get that cad. He is ruining everything! *(PEDRO runs offstage after SILVIO. VICEREINE raises her hand to slap JUANA, but lowers*

it. Coldly:) Is this how you acknowledge my affection? Is this your gratitude?

JUANA. Forgive me, señora, my friend, my dear confidant.

VICEREINE. You are blackening your future.

JUANA. I love him.

VICEREINE. And love brings happiness? You think loving someone brings happiness?

JUANA. Better. It brings freedom.

VICEREINE. It's so like you to want the one thing I don't have to give. You are such a child! A capricious, bullheaded... beautiful child. *(Pause.)* You are leaving then?

JUANA. Yes.

VICEREINE *(pause)*. I suppose I would too, if I could. *(JUANA, touched, hugs the VICEREINE's from behind.)* You know, dear Juana, love and reason are two foreign creatures, opposed, contradictory. The heart may move you to do things you never imagined doing. Passion breaks promises. Love is a tremendous force, the only thing stronger should be the resistance to its loss. Loss of love—loneliness—is the deepest tragedy there is, Juana. And no matter what people, the Viceroy, or God say... no matter how your love is viewed in their narrow eyes... you must do everything—EVERYTHING—not to lose what you have gained.

JUANA. I know.

VICEREINE. One must do what is necessary, my dear. Even if it is difficult.

JUANA. Your understanding is a blessing.

VICEREINE. I only want what is best for you. *(Kisses JUANA's forehead.)* God be with you.

(PEDRO enters breathless.)

PEDRO. The cad got away!

VICEREINE. Silence, Pedro! *(To JUANA.)* Do not worry, my dear, your true love will never leave you. Juana. Now go eat something and lie down, you look so pale

JUANA. Of course. Thank you, señora. *(JUANA exits.)*

PEDRO. The man is a rogue and Juana a ...

VICEREINE. Silence, Don Pedro! You must be respectful of the man Juana loves.*(Pause.)* Which is why, you must be merciful and quick, when you kill him.

PEDRO. I beg your pardon?

VICEREINE. Don Pedro, you must run your blade swiftly when you slice his throat. Or spear that heart of his in two. I will not allow him to destroy that girl's future. Don Silvio, philosopher, nobleman, and Master of Letters, shall not live to see another day. No others shall know about any of this, especially the Viceroy.

PEDRO. Señora, the knave is gone.

VICEREINE. Pedro, do you really think a man like Don Silvio would leave a woman like Juana? He'll be back. You will wait outside with sword in hand.

PEDRO. But Don Silvio is a gifted swordsman. And I have never—

VICEREINE. No time for thoughts. Attack from all sides. Wear down all defenses. Exhaust him. Confuse him. Overpower him. Do you understand, Pedro?

PEDRO. A murder?

VICEREINE *(pause. Aware of the sin she's committing).* Let us just call it: an act of passion. *(VICEREINE exits.)*

PEDRO *(ambivalent).* An errand of weight and dignity ...

(Enter XOCHITL.)

XOCHITL. Forgive me, Don Pedro, I was looking for the Vicereine.

PEDRO. Xochitl! I am glad you are here! Just the person I was looking for.

XOCHITL. Señor?

PEDRO. I have an important errand I must do but I must notify the Viceroy before I leave. *(PEDRO takes out paper and pen and scribbles quickly on the paper.)* Xochitl, can you understand what is written here?

XOCHITL. No, señor.

PEDRO. Good. Take this message to the Viceroy immediately. It involves an affair of state.

XOCHITL. I will deliver it to the appropriate hands.

(XOCHITL exits, PEDRO draws his sword and crosses himself.)

SCENE THREE

AT RISE: *JUANA is in her room, packing. She is more interested in bringing books than clothes. Enter XOCHITL.*

XOCHITL. Juana! Juana Inés! What are you doing?

JUANA. Nothing.

XOCHITL. You have your favorite books all in one bag.

JUANA. The Vicereine is interested in reading them.

XOCHITL *(pulls a brush from the bag)*. Is she interested in using your brush as well?

JUANA *(pulls it away from XOCHITL)*. I knew I had misplaced it.

XOCHITL. Misplaced your head and misplaced your heart, my dear.

JUANA. You think you can read my mind!

XOCHITL. I see what I see... and my eyes do not lie. You are leaving with that Silvio.

JUANA *(pause)*. Perhaps I am.

XOCHITL *(spits on the ground and the floor rumbles)*. Does the Vicereine approve of you wasting your life on the lowest of gamblers?

JUANA. Enough, Xochitl! You know not what you say.

XOCHITL. I know what I can read.

JUANA. Read? Your kind cannot read.

XOCHITL *(pulls out the piece of paper)*. "Dear Honored Sir, It is my duty to inform you that Silvio has fulfilled his portion of the pact: he has aptly seduced Juana Inés. (At this moment, I am searching for Silvio to give him his reward.) Ever faithfully, Pedro." *(Spits. Floor rumbles. Short pause.)* My kind can do anything.

(XOCHITL hands paper to JUANA. JUANA reacts as if all the air has been knocked out of her, she lets out a faint cry. She tears out of the room, discovering PEDRO hiding with his sword.)

JUANA. Don Pedro! *(She surprises him, and disarms him. She picks up his sword.)*

PEDRO. Juana, I objected the moment the Viceroy contemplated this bet.

JUANA. How much did he stand to gain?

PEDRO. I warned you, Juana. I told you to beware.

JUANA. How much?

PEDRO. One thousand reales.

JUANA. To do what? *(Beat.)* I want to know.
PEDRO *(pause)*. To meet you, distract you.
JUANA. I want to know it all.
PEDRO *(pause)*. Juana, how could you fall for that man?
JUANA. I did not fall, Pedro. I leapt. What else was the man supposed to do?
PEDRO. Dishonor you.
JUANA Destroy me.
PEDRO. Render you a woman no longer of worth.
JUANA *(calmly)*. Oh. I see. No longer a woman of worth? *(With rage. She drops the sword.)*
PEDRO. Juana...

JUANA *(hits PEDRO very hard)*.
"Foolhardy men,
Blaming the women you abuse
Not seeing you are the cause
Of the crimes you accuse

Your desire is unequaled
Her disdain will not be had
Why chide her to be good
When you want her to be bad?

She turns away, she gives in
Regardless, you are cruel
If rejected, you complain
If loved, you ridicule.

So who is more at fault
Despite the wrong, therein?

> She, who sins to love,
> Or he who loves to sin?"

JUANA *(pause)*. Don Pedro, when you reward him, give him this. *(Hands PEDRO the gold chain.)*

PEDRO. I've been sent to punish him.

JUANA *(pause. Deliberately picks up the sword and hands it to PEDRO)*. He is hiding at the oak that divides the stream.

PEDRO *(beat)*. Juana.

JUANA. Go! *(PEDRO exits.)*

XOCHITL. What are you doing, Juana?

JUANA. Surviving, Xochitl.

XOCHITL. You know what Don Pedro intends to do! A man with a drawn sword means true harm. The gods will spit on that gambler, but, Juana, you mustn't...

JUANA. A woman should be seen and not heard, fall when pushed, and forgive when betrayed. *(Pause.)* But I am not that type of woman and I discover neither are you.

XOCHITL. I have a life beyond these walls. This room is not the center of my world. I know this violence will not do.

JUANA. It's not violence. It's justice.

XOCHITL. Call the sun the moon, but certain truth will dawn.

JUANA. What truth?

XOCHITL *(provokes wind)*.
> Reason is a sword
> With purpose on both sides
> The base to defend
> The point to make others die

Act II   THE SINS OF SOR JUANA   83

> If, conscious of the danger
> I negotiate the blade,
> Blame not the witless sword
> For the bloody choice I made.

(Pause.) I quote YOU!

JUANA *(beat)*. What have I done? Xochitl, please help me. We must stop Pedro. *(JUANA stumbles.)*

XOCHITL. Look at you, wasting away, *mi'ja*. Shivering. Burning and pale. What will become of you? What will become of us? Why do you break our hearts this way?

JUANA. Xochitl, please go. Go! *(XOCHITL does a native blessing for JUANA and leaves. JUANA walks, grieving, restless.)* Logos. Ethos. Pathos. Logic. Ethics. *(Beat.)* Feelings. I promised I was not going to be like the rest... and here I am, the worst of all.

(JUANA sits down... pulls out paper and pen and furiously begins to write. Time passes. SILVIO appears.)

SILVIO. I waited by the oak and you did not come. *(Beat.)* You found out about the pact. *(No response.)* Don't you understand? I would die for you.

JUANA. You lied to me.

SILVIO. I wish...

JUANA. Wishes are for still and quiet wells and I'm neither. No man's pact, prayer, or promise will shame me into silence. Not even yours.

SILVIO. Don Pedro is dead. *(Beat.)* I never killed a man before. A sound. I called your name. It was Pedro with a sword, and the chain I gave you in his hands. You know

I love you! *(Beat.)* Maybe Pedro was right. Nothing good can come of us.
JUANA. No.
SILVIO. Juana Inés, you and I...we are both...just bastards.
JUANA. No!
SILVIO. I killed Pedro, and you... You loved me. You ennobled me.
JUANA & SILVIO. You betrayed me!

(SILVIO drags JUANA's hand across a deep wound on his side. He holds her open, bloodied palm up to her. SILVIO bends her hand together with both of his and strongly kisses the back of her hand. JUANA realizes he is dying. She backs away.)

JUANA *(softly. Shocked).* No.

(Lights out. SILVIO should not die on stage.)

SCENE FOUR

AT RISE: *VICEREINE is sitting by herself. PADRE NUÑEZ is escorted in by XOCHITL.*

VICEREINE. Padre Nuñez, thank you for coming so quickly.
PADRE. When I heard this was in regards to Juana Inés, I left all my duties.
VICEREINE. Nothing I say seems to help.
XOCHITL. Padre, she will not eat. She will not sleep. She is weak. All she does is sit by candlelight and write.

PADRE. Has she said anything?

VICEREINE. No!   XOCHITL. Yes.

PADRE. Xochitl, what does she say?

XOCHITL *(pause).* All she says... all she asks... is where they buried Silvio.

VICEREINE. Where do they bury the bodies of thieves and scoundrels, the nobodies of this world? Truly, Padre, I know very little about this... other than Don Pedro surprised this charlatan and was forced to use his weapon against him.

XOCHITL. Both men dead for their efforts.

VICEREINE. Don Pedro murdered by the stream. The scoundrel dead in her room. *(Beat.)* The Viceroy is inconsolable; he insisted on a royal burial for his valet.

XOCHITL. And Silvio's body was dragged away by his heels...

VICEREINE. The man had it coming, dishonoring this house like he did. And yet, if I had known Juana would react like she has... I would have never... *(Pause.)* Padre, nothing I say... nothing I do... changes her demeanor. I convinced Don Fabio to still have her, not as his wife, of course, but as a mistress, which under the circumstances is a true gift. And yet... Juana... does not... Padre, I want Juana to look at me again. I want her back from inside her mind. I cannot lose Juana.

PADRE. Has she prayed?

XOCHITL. No, she writes.

PADRE. I wish to speak to her.

(VICEREINE and XOCHITL lead PADRE to JUANA's door; they open it. JUANA is sitting at her desk, slowly writing. She lifts her head. She is not listless. She is silent, in pain, intense. She is aware of everything around her but chooses to ignore what she will.)

VICEREINE. Juana, my dear, Padre Nuñez is here to speak to you. *(JUANA stops writing, but doesn't put down the pen.)* You must be polite, and speak with him. *(Beat.)* Remember, Don Fabio will be coming later, so you might as well develop the habit of speaking again. *(JUANA nods.)*

XOCHITL. Just say something, *mi'ja*.

VICEREINE. Does the devil have your tongue? You will not be allowed to sit in silence, do you understand? You cannot continue doing this to me.

PADRE. Perhaps, it would be best if I were alone with her.

VICEREINE *(hesitates)*. All right. Juana, dear, remember I will always be close by. Come, Agnes.

(XOCHITL and VICEREINE exit. JUANA writes. PADRE paces a moment in silence.)

PADRE. I know where Silvio is. *(JUANA stops writing.)* He is buried in a mass grave not far from the church. *(JUANA puts her pen down.)* The grave is unmarked, except for a nearby bush of wild berries. *(Pause.)* May I read it? *(JUANA allows him to take the paper from her desk. He reads it.)* Juana, this is stunning. Absolutely stunning. *(Pause.)* Your words ... are beautiful.

JUANA *(pause)*. Thank you.

PADRE *(sits down beside her)*. What are you going to do, my child? Are you going to accept Don Fabio's offer?

JUANA *(pause)*. No.

PADRE. Can you return home?

JUANA. I will not go home.

PADRE. Then... *(JUANA picks up the pen and begins to write again. PADRE begins to pull the pen out of her hand.)* Child, you are going to kill yourself like this.

JUANA *(holds onto the pen)*. It is the only thing that is keeping me alive.

PADRE. May I? *(Reaches for another paper and reads it.)*
> We judge
> Yet cannot see
> The sovereign peak
> And humble valley
> Are the same distance from Heaven.

Outstanding. *(Beat.)* So much said, so few words. The imagery. Were I so skilled!

JUANA. Padre, you write.

PADRE. Yes, I do. Some. *(Pause.)* I've rhymed since I was a child. I enjoy verse very much.

JUANA *(pause)*. Padre, I wish to join your convent.

PADRE. Join my convent in a marriage with God? What treasure! Juana, your presence would certainly enrich our days.

JUANA. But, I must be allowed to write.

PADRE. You realize, Juana Inés, that you will be Christ's bride; you will submit to God's will. You will have daily scheduled duties. You cannot leave the convent.

JUANA. As long as I am allowed to write. Every day. *(Beat.)* Padre, can you promise me the daily time and tolerance to put my thoughts and feelings on paper?

PADRE. God has granted you a blessing and a burden. *(Pause.)* In my convent, you will always be allowed to write.

JUANA. Padre, will you be my confessor, my tutor, my protector?

PADRE. My child, I will be your Father.

JUANA *(pause. JUANA kneels and gives him gold chain)*. Forgive me, Father, for I have sinned.

PADRE. Redeem yourself, my child; be true to God.

JUANA. I will be Sor Juana Inés de la Cruz.

(Lights dim. Everything that was colorful and decorative, that resembled the court, is returned into the trunk, taken away. Stark grays. It is now the present again. A sole lit candle. JUANA, dressed in habit, lies with her head on the table. NOVICE is shuffling outside her door.)

JUANA. Who's there? *(No response. JUANA stands and walks over to the door.)* Once again, who is there? *(No response.)* The devil have your tongue? You bring no food, no linen, barely any water. You've taken everything and given nothing. Why would you possibly need to be outside my door?

(NOVICE pushes a stack of paper under the door. JUANA picks it up. She opens the door and is surprised to see the NOVICE who stands with a basket, nervously looking around to see if anyone has seen her. NOVICE scoots in the door past JUANA. JUANA closes the door. Silence. NOVICE places an inkwell and pen on the table.)

NOVICE. For you, Sor Juana. *(JUANA is moved, overwhelmed.)* The paper, the pen. *(Pause.)* They are a gift *(Pause.)* from Father Nuñez. *(Pause.)* He wanted you to have them *(Pause.)* so you could write. *(JUANA looks up.)* Write poems.

JUANA. Father Nuñez has forgiven me?

NOVICE. Padre Nuñez does not want your talent to waste away. But you must eat. You've been twelve days without food. Here, some bread, please.

JUANA *(ignores the food)*. Padre Nuñez will allow me to write again? To write poems?

NOVICE. Yes! *(Pause.)* In honor of the Bishop of Puebla.

JUANA. The Bishop?

NOVICE. In honor of the Church. Padre Nuñez, in his graciousness, gives you these gifts on the condition that, on your promise, he will see what you write. You are to stay within the topic or form that he requests. You are always to share your writing with him. You are to write within the confines of what he ordains appropriate for a woman. And although you are not to publish again, your beautiful poems will honor God.

JUANA. And I can write again?

NOVICE. Yes. *(JUANA gently reaches for the pen and paper and picks up a piece of bread.)* As soon as you destroy the cross-stitch, you...you are free to write again.

(JUANA picks up the cross-stitch. She reads it.)

JUANA. Hand me the instrument.

(NOVICE does. JUANA looks at the cross-stitch again, closes her hand around the blade and runs the knife

along the inside of her palm. Blood drips out of her clenched fist. NOVICE screams:)

NOVICE. Sor Juana!

JUANA *(low and fierce)*. You tell Padre Nuñez that I will not tear out these lines. Tell him that I will not be constrained by what he ordains appropriate for a woman. I have many things wrong but I will not ask forgiveness for my sex or the talent that God granted.

NOVICE. God have mercy. Are you crazy, Sor Juana?

JUANA. Tell *el Padre* I will not write any poems honoring the Bishop, or Earth or Heaven because I never intend to write again. Never.

NOVICE. Sor Juana, be reasonable, Compromise. Padre Nuñez has not altogether prohibited you from...

JUANA. I have "negotiated" on everything that has ever crossed my path...and with every agreement lost a little of myself. And I have hurt others. I have betrayed family, friends, freedom... I have betrayed love. *(She holds up the cross-stitching.)* I will not betray this. Let God hear my testimony, let my words be etched in blood. I, Sor Juana Inés de la Cruz, swear never to write again. *(She presses her palm on the paper and hands the bloodied paper to the NOVICE.)* Listen to my silence. Go tell Padre Nuñez.

(NOVICE takes the paper and scoots away. JUANA walks around the room, wraps her cross-stitching around her wound. She throws the papers on the floor and lowers herself into her chair. She places her head on the table.)

JUANA. I vowed. I vowed. I vowed.

(All the court characters appear: SILVIO, VICEREINE, VICEROY, PEDRO, XOCHITL, in shadows around her.)

JUANA *(looks up)*. Are you not aware that it is a sin for me to speak to the memories of the dead? You are all dead. Gone. *(Laughs bitingly. Pause.)* I have truly lost everything. I vowed... *(Beat.)* I gave my word... *(Beat.)* I am here for a reason! *(ALL CHARACTERS retreat, except SILVIO. He and JUANA lock gazes. Beat.)* Why is Loss the Sacred Price of love? *(SILVIO takes off JUANA's wrapping and kisses the palm of her hurt hand and exits. JUANA watches him go. A wind blows.)*

All could be yours, all could be mine.

If we had lived *(Beat.)* and died.
Different place, different time.

(JUANA returns to her desk. Sits. She instinctively reaches out for her pen. She retracts her hand. She pushes the pen and paper off her desk. She sits and waits.)

God have mercy on our souls.

(JUANA blows out the candle. Rests her head on the table. Lights go down. A light comes up on the NOVICE. She is looking at the paper with JUANA's bloodied handprint. She sets it down, opens a journal and begins to write.)

END OF PLAY

DIRECTOR'S NOTES

DIRECTOR'S NOTES

DIRECTOR'S NOTES

DIRECTOR'S NOTES

DIRECTOR'S NOTES